APOLOGETICS

by

Cornelius Van Til, Th.M., Ph.D.

Professor of Apologetics

Westminster Theological Seminary
Chestnut Hill, Philadelphia, Pa.

PRESBYTERIAN AND REFORMED PUBLISHING CO.
Phillipsburg, New Jersey

CONTENTS

CHAPTER I

THE SYSTEM OF CHRISTIAN TRUTH

Apologetics is the vindication of the Christian philosophy of life against the various forms of the non-Christian philosophy of life.

It is frequently said that apologetics deals with theism, while evidences deals with Christianity. For that reason, it is said, apologetics deals with philosophy while evidences deals with facts.

Now there is, to be sure, a certain amount of truth in this way of putting the matter. Apologetics does deal with theism more than it deals with Christianity, and evidences does deal with Christianity more than it deals with theism. For that reason, too, apologetics deals mostly with philosophy and evidences deals mostly with facts. But the whole matter is a question of emphasis.

That the whole question can be no more than one of emphasis and never one of separation is due to the fact that Christian theism is a unit. Christianity and theism are implied in one another. If we ask, e.g., why Christ came into the world, the answer is that he came to save his people from their sins. But what is sin? It is "Any want of conformity unto, or transgression of, the law of God." And who or what is God?

True, we have here given the orthodox doctrine of the work of Christ, and the orthodox definition of sin. But we could just as well give any other definition of the work of Christ and we should find that it always involves a certain concept of God. If we say that Christ came to set us a fine example of morality and no more, then we have redefined sin to mean some weakness inherent in human nature and therewith we have redefined God to be something less than that absolute and holy being which orthodox theology conceives him to be. Christianity can never be separated from some theory about the existence and the nature of God. The result is that Christian theism must be thought of as a unit.

We may, therefore, perhaps conceive of the vindication of Christian theism as a whole to modern warfare. There is bayonet fighting, there is rifle shooting, there are machine guns, but there are also heavy cannon and atom bombs. All the men engaged in these different kinds of fighting are mutually dependent upon one another. The rifle men could do very little if they did not fight under the protection of the heavy guns behind them. The heavy guns depend for the progress they make upon the smaller guns. So too with Christian theism. It is impossible and useless to seek to vindicate Christianity as a historical religion by a discussion of facts only. Suppose

1

we assert that Christ arose from the grave. We assert further that his resurrection proves his divinity. This is the nerve of the "historical argument" for Christianity. Yet a pragmatic philosopher will refuse to follow this line of reasoning. Granted he allows that Christ actually arose from the grave, he will say that this proves nothing more than that something very unusual took place in the case of "that man Jesus." The philosophy of the pragmatist is to the effect that everything in this universe is unrelated and that such a fact as the resurrection of Jesus, granted it were a fact, would have no significance for us who live two thousand years after him. It is apparent from this that if we would really defend Christianity as an historical religion we must at the same time defend the theism upon which Christianity is based. This involves us in philosophical discussion. To interpret a fact of history involves a philosophy of history. But a philosophy of history is at the same time a philosophy of reality as a whole. Thus we are driven to philosophical discussion all the time and everywhere. Yet in defending the theistic foundation of Christianity we, in the nature of the case, deal almost exclusively with philosophical argument. In apologetics we shoot the big guns under the protection of which the definite advances in the historical field must be made. In short, there is an historical and there is a philosophical aspect to the defense of Christian theism. Evidences deals largely with the historical while apologetics deals largely with the philosophical aspect. Each has its own work to do but they should constantly be in touch with one another.

If we are to defend Christian theism as a unit it must be shown that its parts are really related to one another. We have already indicated the relation between the doctrine of Christ's work, the doctrine of sin, and the doctrine of God. The whole curriculum of an orthodox seminary is built upon the conception of Christian theism as a unit. The Bible is at the center not only of every course, but at the center of the curriculum as a whole. The Bible is thought of as authoritative on everything of which it speaks. Moreover, it speaks of everything. We do not mean that it speaks of football games, of atoms, etc., directly, but we do mean that it speaks of everything either directly or by implication. It tells us not only of the Christ and his work, but it also tells us who God is and where the universe about us has come from. It tells us about theism as well as about Christianity. It gives us a philosophy of history as well as history. Moreover, the information on these subjects is woven into an inextricable whole. It is only if you reject the Bible as the word of God that you can separate the so-called religious and moral instruction of the Bible from what it says, e.g., about the physical universe.

This view of Scripture, therefore, involves the idea that there is nothing in this universe on which human beings can have full and true information unless they take the Bible into account. We do not mean, of course, that one must go to the Bible rather than to the laboratory if one wishes to study the anatomy of the snake. But if one goes only to the laboratory and not also to the Bible one will not have a full or even true interpretation of the snake. Apologetics must therefore take a definitely assigned place in the curriculum of an orthodox seminary. To intimate this place, something must be said about the general subject of theological encyclopedia.

By theological encyclopedia is meant the arrangement in the curriculum of the various theological disciplines. These disciplines are all centered about the Bible because the Bible is thought of as described above. There are first of all the Biblical departments dealing with the Old and New Testaments respectively. In these departments the original languages, exegesis, and Biblical theology are taught. In all this there is a defense as well as a positive statement of the truth. The matter of defense of the truth of Christian theism cannot be left to the apologetic department alone. The specific truths of Christianity must be defended as soon as they are stated. Not one of them has been allowed to stand without attack, and the experts in each field can best defend them. Then comes systematic theology which takes all the truths brought to light from Scripture by the biblical studies and forms them into one organic whole. Of this we must speak more fully in the next section. When we have the system of truth before us we wish to see how it is to be brought to men, and how it has been brought to men. Since it is the word of God, or God's interpretation to men, it must be brought in God's name and with God's authority. In practical theology the matter of preaching the Word is taken up. Here too defense must be coupled with positive statement. Then church history takes up the story as to how this preaching of the Word has fared throughout the centuries. Have those to whom the preaching and teaching of the Word was entrusted brought it faithfully in accordance with the genius of that Word as the Word of God? Have men readily received it when it was preached faithfully? What has been the fruit if it has perhaps been poorly preached and half-heartedly received? Such questions as these will be asked in church history. And again, defense and positive statement go hand in hand.

This really completes the story of Christian encyclopedia. There has been in the disciplines enumerated a detailed and comprehensive statement of the truth. There has been in addition to that a defense of every truth at every point. Is there then no place for apologetics? It would seem so. Yet perhaps there may be the work of a messenger boy. Perhaps the messenger boy can bring the maps and plans of one general to another general. Perhaps the man who is engaged in biblical exegesis is in need of the maps of the whole front as they have been worked out by the man engaged in systematic theology. Perhaps there will be a more unified and better organized defense of Christian theism as a whole if the apologist performs this humble service of a messenger boy. Then too the apologist may be something in the nature of a scout to detect in advance and by night the location and, if possible, something of the movements of the enemy. We use these martial figures of speech because we believe that in the nature of the case the place of apologetics cannot be very closely defined. We have at the outset defined apologetics as the vindication of Christian theism. This is well enough, but we have seen that each discipline must make its own defense. The other disciplines cover the whole field and they offer defense along the whole front. Then too they use the only weapons available to the apologist; namely, philosophical and factual argument. It remains that in apologetics we have no well-delimited field of operation and no exclusive claim to any particular weapon.

The net result then seems to be that in apologetics we have the whole field to cover. And it was this that was included in the analogy of a messenger boy and a scout. This does not imply that the messenger boy or the scout must leave all the work of defense to the others so that he would have nothing to do but carry news from one to the other. No indeed, the scout carries a rifle when he goes scouting in the historical field. Then too he may have to and does have to use the large stationary guns that command a larger distance.

We have just now employed the figure of a fortress or citadel. We may think of the apologist as constantly walking up and down on or near the outer defenses of the fortress. This will give the other occupants time to build and also enjoy the building. The others too must defend, but not so constantly and unintermittently. The apologist too must rest and must enjoy the peace of the fort but his main work is to defend and vindicate.

In this connection we must guard against a misuse that might be made of the figure of the fortress. It might be argued that this seems to put Christianity on the defensive. Is it not true that Christianity was meant to conquer the whole world for Christ? Yes it is. We have already said that we think of Christian theism, when we think of Christianity. That covers the whole earth. If we can successfully defend the fortress of Christian theism we have the whole world to ourselves. There is then no standing room left for the enemy. We wage offensive as well as defensive warfare. The two cannot be separated. But we need not leave the fort in order to wage offensive warfare.

SYSTEMATIC THEOLOGY

It is apparent from our discussion so far that Systematic Theology is more closely related to apologetics than are any of the other disciplines. In it we have the system of truth that we are to defend. We must therefore look briefly at this system which we are offered.

Systematics divides what it has to give us into six divisions as follows: theology, anthropology, Christology, soteriology, ecclesiology, and eschatology. We shall look at each of these in turn.

A. THEOLOGY

Naturally, in the system of theology and in apologetics the doctrine of God is of fundamental importance. In apologetics it must always be the final if not the first point of attack. In theology the main questions deal with the existence and the nature of God. We ask the questions "Does God exist?"

and "What kind of God is he?" Frequently the order in which the various questions pertaining to the doctrine of God are taken up is that of the knowability of God, the existence of God, and the nature of God. For our purposes, however, we may begin with the question of the nature of God. We are not interested in discussing the existence of a God the nature of whom we do not know. We must first ask what kind of a God Christianity believes in before we can really ask with intelligence whether such a God exists. The what precedes the that; the connotation precedes the denotation; at least the latter cannot be discussed intelligently without at once considering the former.

What do we mean when we use the word God? Systematics answers this question in its discussion of the attributes or properties of God. We mention only those that pertain to God's being, his knowledge, and his will.

The Being of God

1. The independence or aseity of God. By this is meant that God is in no sense correlative to or dependent upon anything beside his own being. God is not even the source of his own being. The term source cannot be applied to God. God is absolute (John 5:26; Acts 17:25). He is sufficient unto himself.

2. The immutability of God. Naturally God does not and cannot change since there is nothing besides his own eternal being on which he depends (Malachi 3:6; James 1:17).

3. The unity of God. As independent and unchangeable God has unity within himself. We distinguish here between the unity of singularity (singularitatis) and the unity of simplicity (simplicitatis). The unity of singularity has reference to numerical oneness. There is and can be only one God. The unity of simplicity signifies that God is in no sense composed of parts or aspects that existed prior to himself (Jer. 10:10; I John 1:5). The attributes of God are not to be thought of otherwise than as aspects of the one simple original being; the whole is identical with the parts. On the other hand the attributes of God are not characteristics that God has developed gradually; they are fundamental to his being; the parts together form the whole. The unity and the diversity in God are equally basic and mutually dependent upon one another. The importance of this doctrine for apologetics may be seen from the fact that the whole problem of philosophy may be summed up in the question of the relation of unity to diversity; the so-called problem of the one and the many receives a definite answer from the doctrine of the simplicity of God.

Man cannot partake of these attributes of God. Man cannot in any sense be the source of his own being; man cannot in any sense be immutable or simple. God's being with its attributes is self-contained. God cannot communicate his being.

5

The Knowledge of God

The question of the nature of the knowledge of God is of the utmost importance in apologetics. God knows his own being to its very depths in one eternal act of knowledge. There are no hidden depths in the being of God that he has not explored. In the being of God, therefore, possibility is identical with reality and potentiality is identical with actuality. In this respect the knowledge of God is wholly different from ours. We can never know the full depth of our being. With us potentiality must always be deeper than actuality. God's knowledge is as incommunicable as is his being. God's knowledge is what it is because his being is what it is.

Should we speak of this knowledge that God has of himself as analytical or as synthetical? The answer depends on what we mean by these terms. In laboratory work we mean by analytical knowledge that which has been acquired by tearing something into its constitutive elements, while by synthetic knowledge we mean that knowledge which we have by virtue of a comprehensive vision of a thing. In the history of philosophy, however, these words have come very near to having the opposite meaning. Especially since the time of Kant, analysis has come to mean that knowledge by which we look within ourselves without reference to the spatio-temporal facts beyond us. It seems then that we must choose between the scientific and the philosophical use of the term. Or must we first see how theologians have used the terms and disregard the others?

Theology has been disposed to use what we have called the scientific use of the terms. So for instance in the history of Protestant theology there has been an argument chiefly between Lutherans, at least since Calixtus' day, and the Calvinists as to where one should start when reasoning about the question of predestination. The Lutherans argued that we must begin with the historical facts of the Christian's experience and then reason back to the idea of predestination. Calixtus called this the analytical method while the method generally followed by the Calvinists, namely that of beginning with the doctrine of God, was called the synthetic method.

All this being as it is, we believe that it is best to speak of God's knowledge of himself as analytical. This does not mean that God must by a slow process analyze himself, but it emphasizes that which most needs emphasis, namely, that God does not need to look beyond himself for additions to his knowledge. This usage will most easily bring us into contact with the philosophical systems that are opposed to Christianity.

Turning now to the second aspect of God's knowledge, i.e., that knowledge which God has of the things that exist beside himself, we must emphasize the fact that God's knowledge of the facts precedes these facts. By this we do not mean temporal precedence. By God's foreknowledge we do not mean that God knows the thing before it occurs. Of course, from the human

6

point of view this is the exact truth of the matter. But we are now looking at the matter from the point of view of God's being, and from this point of view the main thing to note is that God's knowledge logically precedes the realization of the facts. We must know or interpret the facts after we look at the facts, after they are there and perhaps after they have operated for some time. But God's knowledge of the facts comes first. God knows or interprets the facts before they are facts. It is God's plan, God's comprehensive interpretation of the facts that makes the facts what they are. Thus God's knowledge of created things is also analytical in the sense defined above.

The Will of God

The will of God is what it is because the being and the knowledge of God are what they are. God is self-sufficient or self-contained in his being. He therefore knows himself and all created existence by a single internal act of intuition. His existence of being is, to its utmost depths, a self-conscious existence. In his being and knowledge God may be said to be purely active. God's own being is therefore the only ultimate object of his own knowledge. Similarly God's being, with all the fulness of its holy attributes, is the only ultimate object of his will. God wills himself in all that he wills. God wants to maintain all his attributes in all their glory. He is the final or highest goal of all that he does. God seeks and establishes his own glory in all that he does.

Two aspects of God's will may here be distinguished. These aspects correspond to two aspects of God's knowledge. God knows himself and he knows the created universe. So too God wills himself and also wills the created universe. When the created universe is not in view at all it is said that God directly knows and wills himself with all his attributes. But when the created universe is in view it must still be said that in knowing and willing it God knows and wills himself. God wills, that is, creates the universe. God wills, that is, by his providence controls the course of development of the created universe and brings it to its climax. Throughout all this he wills, that is, he seeks, his glory. He seeks his glory. He seeks it, and seeking it sees to it that his purpose in seeking it is accomplished. No creature can detract from his glory; all creatures, willingly or unwillingly, add to his glory. Thus God wills himself in and through his will with respect to created reality. Whatever God wills with respect to the created universe is a means to what he wills with respect to himself.

Summing up what has been said about God's being, knowledge and will, it may be said that God's being is self-sufficient, his knowledge is analytical and his will is self-referential. In his being, knowledge and will God is self-contained. There is nothing correlative to him. He does not depend in his being, knowledge, or will upon the being, knowledge, or will of his own creatures. God is absolute. He is autonomous.

7

The Triune Personal God

In what has been said it is the triune personal God of Scripture that is in view. God exists in himself as a triune self-consciously active being. The Father, the Son, and the Holy Ghost are each a personality and together constitute the exhaustively personal God. There is an eternal, internal self-conscious interaction between the three persons of the Godhead. They are co-substantial. Each is as much God as are the other two. The Son and the Spirit do not derive their being from the Father. The diversity and the unity in the Godhead are therefore equally ultimate; they are exhaustively correlative to one another and not correlative to anything else.

It is customary to speak of the Trinity as thus described as the ontological Trinity. The ontological Trinity must be distinguished from the economical Trinity. By the latter is meant the distinction of persons within the Godhead in so far as this distinction has bearing on the works of God with respect to the created universe. The Father is centrally active in the creation and sustaining of the universe. The Son is centrally active in the objective work of salvation. The Spirit is centrally active in the subjective work of salvation. In all this the triune God is active with respect to the universe. But when God is contemplated as active within himself, we speak of the ontological Trinity.

What has been said about the being, knowledge, and will of God, as the being, knowledge, and will of the self-sufficient ontological Trinity may suffice for purposes of introduction. Enough has been said to set off the Christian doctrine of God clearly from the various forms of the non-Christian doctrine of God. The God of Christianity alone is self-contained and self-sufficient. He remains so even when he stands in relation to the world as its creator and sustainer. All other gods are either out of all relation to the universe or else correlative to it.

The Christian teaching of the ontological Trinity, therefore, gives it a clearly distinguishable metaphysic, epistemology and ethic. In all these three Christian theism is wholly different from any other philosophy of life.

Christian Metaphysics

God has one kind of being, being that is infinite, eternal, and unchangeable and full of holy attributes. The universe has another sort of being, being that has been produced and is sustained by God. In contrast with this, all non-Christian forms of metaphysics speak of being in general, being as such. They claim to be able to make intelligible assertions about the nature of being in general. Or if they do not claim to be able to do this they assume that such can be done. So, for instance, Aristotle speaks of the nature of being in general and affirms that it is analogical in character. He introduces the distinction between kinds of being, such as divine being and human being after he has made certain assertions about the nature of being in general. But thus to make assertions about being in general constitutes, by implication at least, an attack upon the self-contained and therefore unique nature of God's being. A position is best known by the most basic distinctions that it makes. The most basic distinction of Christianity is that of God's being as self-contained, and created being as dependent upon him. Christianity is committed for better or for worse to a two-layer theory of reality or being. All non-Christian theories of being would call this position of Christian theism dualistic. Of this we shall need to speak later. For the moment it is important that the basic concepts of Christianity be clearly set off from other views. And the doctrine of God's being as qualitatively distinct from every other form of being is characteristic of Christianity alone. From the Christian point of view all other forms of metaphysical theory hold to a monistic assumption.

The position of the Roman Catholic church on this point may at once be noted. While claiming to hold to the Christian theory of reality Thomas Aquinas and his modern followers in effect follow Aristotle in speaking first of being in general and in introducing the distinction between divine being and created being afterwards. The consequences are fatal both for systematic theology and for apologetics. For systematic theology it means that God is not unequivocally taken to be the source of man's being and the controlling power over his actions. Every doctrine is bound to be false if the first and basic doctrine of God is false. For apologetics it means that the non-Christian forms of metaphysics cannot be challenged in their basic assumptions. Not believing in the scriptural doctrine of the self-contained being of God, Romanism cannot offer this God as the final reference point for all human predication. Of this also we shall speak more fully later.

Christian Epistemology

Herewith we have already come to the question of epistemology. As God has self-contained being and all other being has created or derivative being, so also God has self-contained and man has derivative knowledge. In contrast with this all forms of non-Christian epistemology speak first of knowledge in general and introduce the distinction between divine and human knowledge afterwards. It is true that there are forms of non-Christian epistemology that speak of the divine knowledge as though it were wholly other, qualitatively different, from human knowledge. So there are also forms of non-Christian metaphysics that speak of God's being as wholly other, as qualitatively different, from man's being. This is notably the case with the Theology of Crisis, informed as it is by a sceptical theory of knowledge. But when this God, whose being and knowledge is said to be so wholly different from the being and knowledge of man is, as he must be, brought into contact with the being and knowledge of man, there follows a fusion of the two. Either God's being and knowledge are brought down to the level of the being and knowledge of man or the being and knowledge of man are lifted up to the being and knowledge of God. There is always

9

the same monistic assumption at work reducing all distinctions to correlatives of one another.

On the question of epistemology as on that of metaphysics the Roman Catholic church again occupies a straddling position. With non-Christian forms of epistemology in general, and with Aristotle in particular, its most basic concept is that of knowledge in general. This is naturally involved in the Aristotelian idea of being in general. Roman Catholicism not only admits but it maintains that Aristotle was right in assuming that it is possible to say something intelligible about being in general. Accordingly it follows Aristotle in speaking of the requirements to which knowledge in general must answer if it is to be true with Aristotle. Romanism assumes that God and man stand in exactly the same sort of relation to the law of contradiction. To think and know truly it is assumed, both must think in accordance with that law as an abstraction from the nature of either. The consequences are again fatal both for systematic theology and apologetics. For systematic theology it means that truth is not made ultimately to consist in correspondence to the internally self-complete nature and knowledge that God has of himself and of all created reality. Hence man's dealings in the realm of truth are not ultimately with God but with an abstraction that stands above God, with Truth as such. For apologetics it means that the basic principle of the non-Christian conception of truth cannot be challenged. According to this most basic assumption it is man rather than God that is the final reference point in all predication. The idea of Truth in the abstract is in accord with this assumption. In fact the idea of truth in the abstract is based upon this assumption.

A moment's reflection upon the fall of man in paradise will prove this to be true. In paradise God said to man that if he ate of the forbidden fruit he would surely die. The truth about the facts in the created universe, Adam and Eve were told in effect, could be known ultimately only if one knew their relationship to the plan of God. It is this plan of God that makes all created facts to be what they are. Granted that man's activity with respect to many facts is a factor in making them what they are, even so it remains true that back of everything that man might do it is ultimately God's plan that is all-controlling. And this plan is in accord with the being or nature of God. God did not, because he could not, look up to an abstract principle of Truth above himself in order, in accordance with it, to fashion the world. Satan, however, suggested to Eve that God's statement about the relation of one temporal fact to another was not determinative of the nature of that relationship. Facts and the truth about their relationships to one another can be known by man, Satan contended in effect, without getting any information about them from God as their maker and controller. How can they thus be known? In the first place, by observation. But observation is not sufficient. Man needed to know something about the future. God pretended to interpret the future relationships of temporal facts to one another. In rejecting God's interpretation of the future relationship of temporal facts to one another man could only rest upon the powers of logical thought within himself. Mere observation of facts would not help him to offer a substitute prediction for that of God for there was as yet no past. So man had to depend upon his powers of logic alone. And he had to assume that these powers could somehow legislate for what is to be in the future. He had, in short, to assume that his powers of logic could legislate for what is possible and impossible in reality about him. He had to say in effect that what God said would come about could not possibly come about. And he had to find this power of legislation exclusively within himself. He had as yet no experience about the course of nature. He could appeal to no law of truth in any objective sense. He had to choose between taking the divine mind or his own mind as the source of truth about all facts. Truth out of all relationship to any mind is a pure meaningless abstraction.

Now Roman Catholicism, bound as it is to its most basic notion of supposedly intelligent predication about being in general, is unable to place this alternative before men. It cannot challenge those who make man the center of their interpretation of life with a view that makes God the center of the interpretation of life.

Christian Ethics

On the question of ethics the doctrine of the self-contained God implies that God's will is the final and exclusively determinative power of whatsoever comes to pass. As already noted, the nature of any created thing is what it is because of an act of determination with respect to it on the part of God. Created things are not identical with God nor with any act of God with respect to them. They have a being and an activity of their own. But this being and activity is what it is because of the more ultimate being and activity on the part of the will of God. Things are what they are ultimately because of the plan of God. They are what they are in relation to one another because of the place that God has assigned them in his plan. God expresses his plan with respect to the facts and laws of nature in these facts and laws themselves. The regularity of the laws of nature is due to the "obedience" of the facts of the created world to the behest of God. True, the word "obedience" can be applied to the laws of nature only in a metaphorical sense. But it helps to express the idea that these laws do not have their regularity in and of themselves without any act of God with respect to them. All force in the created universe acts in accordance with the forthputting of the power of God that is back of it.

The particular case of the will of man in relation to the will of God calls for a brief remark in this connection. To begin with the will of man as an aspect of this personality depends for what it is ultimately upon a creative and sustaining act of God, but the will of man as an aspect of human personality is not observable except in act. For man as bound to act, God has set his program. God gave this program by way of self-conscious com-

11

munication at the beginning of history. Man's summum bonum was set before him, individually and collectively. He was to subdue the earth and bring out its latent powers to the glory of God. He was to be a willing servant of God, one who would find his delight in obedience to God. His criterion for action would be faith in the truth of promises of God.

If obedient to the will of God, man would be accomplishing genuine results. The controlling and directing power of his will would be the will of God. It would be by his own will, however, that he would reach the goal that God has set for him. If disobedient to the will of God he would be going counter to the expressed will of God for him. Yet he would not be able to frustrate the plan of God either as a whole or in any detail. Man as a creature cannot will anything either by way of obedience or by way of disobedience except in a relation of subordination to the plan of God. It is the ultimate will or plan of the self-determinate God that gives determinate character to anything that is done by the human will.

Over against this Christian view of the will of God as ultimate is the non-Christian view of the will of man as ultimate. Morality is assumed to be autonomous. Man is virtually said to be a law unto himself. He may, and in many cases does, speak of God as his law-giver. But then this God is a projection of his own ultimate moral consciousness; God is but man's would-be ultimate and autonomous moral consciousness writ large. Socrates wanted to know what "the holy" was apart from what any man or God might say about it. This might seem to point to an "objective" holiness quite apart from the consciousness of man. But such a holiness apart from the consciousness of man is devoid of meaning. There is no alternative to the Christian view of the will of God as ultimate but the idea of man's moral consciousness itself as being ultimate. In modern times the categorical imperative of Kant is a good illustration of the would-be autonomous nature of non-Christian ethics. It is therefore the business of Christian apologetics to challenge the non-Christian view of morality and to show that unless the will of God be taken as ultimate there is no meaning to moral distinctions.

The Roman Catholic view of ethics is unable to do this. It has been noted that Romanism virtually speaks of being in general and of knowledge in general before it speaks of the being and knowledge of God as distinct from the being and knowledge of man. It is natural then that God's will cannot be made primary in ethics. Roman Catholic theology ascribes to the will of man such a measure of autonomy and ultimacy as to enable it to determine man's own final destiny whether for good or for evil requiring only the assistance of God. For Romanism man is himself the ultimate source of his own determinateness. To be sure, Romanism tones down this teaching of man's autonomy by also teaching the "almighty" character of God's will. For all that Romanism is jealous for the ultimacy of the will of man.

The consequences of this position for systematic theology and apologetics are again far-reaching. For systematic theology it means that the initiative is taken out of God's hand at every point of doctrine. The doctrine of creation becomes a cross between the Christian doctrine of creation out of nothing and the pagan doctrine of the chain of being. The doctrine of salvation becomes a matter of give and take between God and man; man is saved partially by grace and partially by works. For apologetics it means that the natural man is not challenged to forsake his disobedience to God in order to find rest for his soul and significance in his moral distinctions. Roman Catholic ethics seeks to by-pass the will of God in order to appeal to his nature. But this in effect amounts to an appeal to the fitness of things in general. Such a notion of the fitness of things in general is in accord with the idea of being and knowledge in general. One who seeks to make intelligent predication about being in general allows in effect that one who does not make the creator-creature distinction basic in his thought can yet make true assertions about reality. Accordingly Romanism admits that non-Christian ethicists can truly determine the nature of the so-called cardinal virtues. Romanism allows that the natural man who makes himself the final reference point of moral distinctions can say what is true about man's proper behavior with respect to many things in this world. Thus Romanism grants in effect that those who do not handle all things in this world in obedience to the will of God and for the glory of God are yet doing what is right. Nor are they merely admitting that the natural man can do what is right as far as the matter of the thing apart from its motivation is concerned. Romanism admits that the natural man who makes himself the goal of his efforts, who uses his own experience instead of the will of God as the criterion of his undertakings and who has not faith as the motivation of all that he does, is yet able to do what is right without qualification in certain areas of life. And this fact disqualifies Romanism from either stating or defending a true Christian doctrine of human behavior.

For our present purposes the doctrine of God need not be set forth more fully. It has appeared that in the Christian doctrine of the self-contained ontological Trinity we have the foundation concept of a Christian theory of being, of knowledge and of action. Christians are interested in showing to those who believe in no God or in a God, a beyond, some ultimate or absolute, that it is this God in whom they must believe lest all meaning should disappear from human words. Christians are interested in showing to those who hold that "God" possibly or probably exists but possibly or probably does not exist, that the words possibility and probability have no meaning unless the God of Christianity actually exists. It is their conviction that the actuality of the existence of this God is the presupposition of all possible predication.

We have now before us, in bare outline, the main points in the Christian doctrine of God. Christianity offers the triune God, the absolute personality containing all the attributes enumerated as the God in whom we be-

13

lieve. This conception of God is the foundation of everything else that we hold dear. Unless we can believe in this sort of God it does us no good to be told that we may believe in any other sort of God or in anything else. For us everything else depends for its meaning upon this sort of God. Accordingly we are not interested in having any one prove to us the existence of any other sort of God than this God. Any other sort of God is no God at all and to prove that some other sort of God exists is to prove that no God exists.

B. ANTHROPOLOGY

The whole question with which we deal in apologetics is one of the relation between God and man. Hence next to the doctrine of God the doctrine of man is of fundamental importance.

1. The image of God in man

Man is created in God's image. He is therefore like God, in everything in which a creature can be like God. He is like God in that he is a personality. This is what we mean when we speak of the image of God in the wider or more general sense. Then when we wish to emphasize the fact that man resembles God especially in the splendor of his moral attributes we add that when man was created he had true knowledge, true righteousness and true holiness. This doctrine is based upon the fact that in the New Testament we are told that Christ came to restore us to true knowledge, righteousness and holiness (Col. 3:10; Eph. 4:24). Christ came to restore and supplement what man had and was in paradise. We call this the image of God in the narrower sense. These two cannot be completely separated from one another. It would really be impossible to think of man's having been created only with the image of God in the wider sense; every act of man would from the very first have to be a moral act, an act of choice for or against God. Hence man would, even in every act of knowledge, manifest true righteousness and true holiness. The idea of disinterested or neutral knowledge is out of accord with the basic ideas of Christianity.

Then after emphasizing that man was created like God and in the nature of the case had to be like God, we must stress the point that man must always be different from God. Man was created in God's image. Man can never in any sense outgrow his creaturehood. This puts a definite connotation into the expression that man is like God. He is like God, to be sure, but always on a creaturely scale. For that reason the church has embedded into the heart of its confessions the doctrine of the incomprehensibility of God. God's being and knowledge are absolutely original; such being and knowledge is too wonderful for man; he cannot attain unto it. Man was created finite and his finitude was originally not felt to be a burden to him. Man could never expect to attain to comprehensive knowledge in the future. We cannot expect to have comprehensive knowledge even in heaven.

It is true that much will be revealed to us that is now a mystery to us, but in the nature of the case God cannot reveal to us that which as creatures we cannot comprehend; we should have to be God ourselves in order to understand God in the depth of his being. Man can understand God's revelation only promensura humana.

The significance of this point will appear more fully when we contrast this conception of mystery with the non-Christian conception of mystery that is current today even in Christian circles. The difference between the Christian and the non-Christian conception of mystery may be expressed in a word by saying that Christians hold that there is mystery for man but not for God, while non-Christians hold that there is either no mystery for God or man or that there is mystery for both God and man.

2. Man's relation to the universe

Next to noting that man was created in God's image it must be observed that man was organically related to the universe about him. Man was to be prophet, priest, and king under God in this created world. The vicissitudes of the world would to a large extent depend upon the deeds of man. As a prophet man was to interpret this world after God, as a priest he was to dedicate this world to God, and as a king he was to rule over it for God. In opposition to this all non-Christian theories hold that the vicissitudes of man and the universe about him are only accidentally and incidentally related.

3. The fall of man

The fall of man needs emphasis as much as does his creation. Man was once upon a time created by God in the image of God. Soon thereafter he fell into sin. As a creature of God man had to live in accordance with the law of God, that is, in accordance with the ordinances that God had placed in his creation. This law was for the most part not verbally transmitted to man but was created in his being. Man would act in accord with his own true nature only if he would obey the law of God and, vice versa, if he would live in accord with his own nature, he would obey the law of God. True, God did communicate to man over and above what was embedded in his very nature the specific commandment not to eat of the tree of the knowledge of good and evil. But this was only to force an immediate and final test as to whether a man would really live in accordance with the law of God as everywhere revealed within and about him.

When man fell it was therefore an attempt to do without God in every respect. Man sought his ideals of truth, goodness and beauty somewhere beyond God, either directly within himself or indirectly within the universe about him. Originally man had interpreted the universe under the direction of God but now he sought to interpret the universe without reference to God. We mean, of course, without reference to the kind of God defined above.

Man made for himself a false ideal of knowledge, the ideal of absolute inderivative comprehension. This he could never have done if he had continued to recognize that he was a creature. It is totally inconsistent with the idea of creatureliness that man should strive for comprehensive knowledge; if it could be attained it would wipe God out of existence; man would then be God. And, as we shall see later, because man sought this unnattainable ideal he brought upon himself no end of woe.

In conjunction with man's false ideal of knowledge we may mention here the fact that when man saw he could not attain his own false ideal of knowledge he blamed this to his finite character. Man confused finitude with sin. Thus he commingled the metaphysical and the ethical aspects of reality. Not willing to take the blame for sin, man laid it to circumstances round about him or within him. Over against this biblical view of man, the non-Christian view assumes or asserts that man is neither created nor sinful in the sense described. Even though much stress is laid upon the fact that man is finite and evil (cf. Barth, Brunner, Niehbuhr) yet man is taken to be his own ultimate reference point. Man virtually occupies the place which the ontological Trinity occupies in orthodox theology. He is self-sufficient and autonomous.

It is only when this point is carefully noted that the Christian and the non-Christian points of view are seen in their right relationship to one another. The two positions have mutually exclusive views of the ultimate reference point in predication.

Roman Catholic apologetics is unable to make this point clear. As already noted it does not make the creator-creature distinction basic in its thought. It has therefore a half-Christian and half non-Christian view of God. Similarly it has a half-Christian and half non-Christian view of man. According to Romanism, man's being is not exclusively described in terms of the general concept of the chain of being. Man is said to have less being than God. He is said to hover near the edge of non-being. Hovering near the edge of non-being and therefore having but little being he is said to tend to slip into non-being. Thus man's "sinfulness" is described in part in terms of the law status he occupies in the scale of being. Because of the attenuated character of his being he tends to evil. Is then God responsible for creating man with so thin a stream of being? The answer is in the negative. But the reason why God is excused from making man evil is that man's being is not exclusively derived from God. The nature of "being in general" controls and limits God in the creation of man. God cannot give man stable being because being is already defined as unstable at the point where man is to be placed. The nature of "being in general" is first defined in indeterminist terms and then God is made to fit into the picture.

16

If man is to exist at all he must be placed at the lower end of the scale of being. Then, being placed there at the same time constitutes his "freedom." For his "freedom" consists in the fact of the unstable nature of his being.

In the field of knowledge the Romanist view of man involves both rationalism and irrationalism. These correspond to determinism and indeterminism in the realm of being. The Roman Catholic apologist will make his final appeal to "knowledge in general" instead of to the self-conscious ontological Trinity. He will try to prove the existence of God by the method of Aristotle, i.e., by showing that God's existence is in accord with "Logic in general." So doing he does not prove the existence of the ontological Trinity; he "proves" the existence of a god, a god that fits into the pattern of "being in general." And he will "prove" that this God "probably" exists; for man has no experience of any sort of being except such as lies at the edge of non-being. Thus Romanism cannot challenge the interpretations of the non-Christian. Seeking to appeal to the "reason" of the natural man, as the natural man himself interprets his reason, the Roman Catholic apologist falls victim both to the rationalism and the irrationalism inherent in the non-Christian view of life.

In the field of ethics the Romanist view involves both dictatorship and autonomy. These correspond to determinism and indeterminism in the field of being and to rationalism and irrationalism in the field of knowledge. The average man is virtually said to be properly subject in an absolute sense (papal authority) to such of their fellow men as have attained to a higher position than have they in the scale of being. The relationship between those in authority and those under authority is not exclusively or even primarily ethical but metaphysical. The Pope, to be sure, speaks for Christ, on Christ's authority, but the only Christ he knows is one who, though God as well as man, yet fits into a certain position in the scale of being. Thus even the Pope deals not exclusively or primarily with the Creator-Redeemer but with "being in general" and "knowledge in general." He derives his authority not primarily from revelation given him by Christ but from his supposedly superior insight into the proper proportions within the scale of being. He is an "expert" in the realm of religion. The average man must listen to him as to a dictator.

On the other hand, the average man cannot through the Pope hear the imperative voice of God at all. "Being in general" and "knowledge in general" have in them an element of ultimate contingency. God himself has no control over the lower reaches of being. These lower reaches of being, though very attenuated, yet have in them a potentiality all their own. God could therefore not make man perfect. There was a sort of "matter" with a refractory power which made it impossible for God to make man perfect. True, Romanism asserts that God made man perfect. But its notion of "being in general" prevents its putting truly Christian meaning into these words. In consequence man's dealings in ethics are not exclusively or primarily with the expressed will of God but with "morality in general." Thus the idea of autonomy, which constitutes the heart of non-Christian ethics, cannot be challenged in Romanist views.

C. CHRISTOLOGY

We now have the two points between which the knowledge transaction takes place. Yet since sin has come into the world we cannot see the whole of the picture of the Christian point of view until we see how God and man are brought together after their separation. The only way they could be brought together again would be if God should bring about salvation for man and therewith reunion with God. Christ came to bring man back to God.

To do this he was and had to be truly God. For that reason the church has emphasized the fact that Christ was a divine, not a human, person. It was the second person of the ontological Trinity who was, in respect of his essence, fully equal with the Father, who therefore existed from all eternity with the Father, who in the incarnation assumed a human nature.

This does not mean that he laid aside his divine nature. It does not mean that he became a human person. It does not mean that he became a divine-human person. It does not mean that the divine and human natures were intermingled. Christ was and remained, even when he was in the manger in Bethlehem, a divine person, but this divine person took to itself in close union with its divine nature a human nature. The Chalcedon creed has expressed all this by saying that in Christ the divine and the human natures are so related as to be unconfusedly, unchangeably, indivisibly and inseparably related. The former two adjectives safeguard the true doctrine against the idea that the divine and the human should in any sense be intermingled; the latter two adjectives safeguard the true doctrine against the idea that there should not be a real union because of the insistence upon distinctness in the former two.

It will be noted at this point that this view of the incarnation is in full accord with the doctrine of God and man as above set forth. If Christ is really the second person of the ontological Trinity he shares in the attributes of the Godhead. On the other hand his human nature was that of a creature of God. Accordingly even in the incarnation Christ could not commingle the eternal and the temporal. The eternal must always remain independent of and prior to the temporal.

In addition to this brief statement about the person of Christ a word must be said about his offices.

Christ is true prophet, priest, and king. The Westminster shorter catechism asks, "How does Christ execute the office of a Prophet?" The

18

answer is: "Christ executeth the office of a Prophet, in revealing to us by His Word and Spirit, the will of God for our salvation." Man set for himself a false ideal of knowledge when he became a sinner, that is, he lost true wisdom. In Christ man was reinstated to true knowledge. In Christ man realizes that he is a creature of God and that he should not seek underived comprehensive knowledge. Christ is our wisdom. He is our wisdom not only in the sense that he tells us how to get to heaven. He is our wisdom too in teaching us true knowledge about everything about which we should have knowledge.

Again the catechism asks: "How does Christ execute the office of a Priest?" The answer is : "Christ executeth the office of a Priest in his once offering up himself a sacrifice to satisfy divine justice, and reconcile us to God, and making continual intercession for us." We need not discuss this point except to indicate that Christ's work as priest cannot be separated from his work as prophet . Christ could not give us true knowledge of God and of the universe unless he died for us as priest. The question of knowledge is an ethical question. It is indeed possible to have theoretically correct knowledge about God without loving God. The devil illustrates this point. Yet what is meant by knowing God in Scripture is knowing and loving God: this is true knowledge of God; all other knowledge of God is false.

In the third place the catechism asks: "How does Christ execute the office of a King?" The answer is: "Christ executeth the office of a King, in subduing us to himself, in ruling and defending us, and in restraining and conquering all of his and our enemies." Again we observe that this work of Christ as King must be brought into organic connection with his work as Prophet and Priest. To give us true wisdom or knowledge Christ must subdue us. He died for us to subdue us and thus gave us wisdom. It is only by emphasizing this organic connection of the aspects of the work of Christ that we can avoid all mechanical separation of the intellectual and the moral in the question of knowledge.

The "Christ" of non-Christian thought is a projection of the would-be autonomous man. This "Christ" may even be said to be "wholly other" as the God of non-Christian thought is sometimes said to be "wholly other." He is then said to give objective revelation of God and to speak with authority for and in the name of God. Even so he is essentially nothing but a projection from the mind of man. He is the ideal which man sets before himself.

Since this Christ is projected into the heights he is said to have "become flesh," to have humiliated himself, even unto death. But this humiliation unto death is in the interest of man's exaltation. And so it is asserted that "in Christ" all men are saved.

19

It will be noted that in this view it is reality as a whole, inclusive of Christ and man, that constitutes the subject of predication. It is this reality as a whole that undergoes a process. According to Barth the whole God, the wholly other God, dies with man and then lifts man, mankind, out of death with himself.

On this essentially monistic scheme man remains his own prophet, priest and king. The work of Christ, both in the state of his humiliation and in the state of his exaltation is the work of man himself. He merely uses the idea of Christ and God as an ideal in order by it to realize his own ideals. And those ideals have their beginning and end in man himself.

The Roman Catholic view of Christ is, as may be expected, a cross between this non-Christian and the Christian view. In so far as the idea of ''being in general'' controls its thought the Romanist view cannot be true to the Chalcedon creed. It must and does virtually confuse the two natures of Christ. As a result the work of Christ as prophet, priest and king is also toned down till it greatly resembles the position of the non-Christian described above. As a prophet Christ cannot speak with authority for God and as God. He is not self-interpretative. He cannot be self-interpretative because he does not control the whole of reality. Being is what it is to some extent without relation to him as God. So he cannot speak through the finished canon of Scripture. Or if he does, this speaking must be mediated to man through the ''living voice'' of the Church. That is to say, it must be mediated through the voice of the Pope as the one who has expert insight into the nature of being in general.

As a priest Christ cannot offer a finished sacrifice to satisfy divine justice; ''being in general'' has in it such measure of contingency that no such finished sacrifice can be offered. The sacrifice of Christ must therefore be a process, a part of the process of being in general.

As a king Christ cannot rule over us and defend us except through the ''living voice'' of authority speaking in the church. The failure to make the creator-creature distinction basic in its thinking results in an obstruction of the imperative voice of God. The creature is not clearly confronted with his God in Romanist theology. So the orders of God do not reach him in unmistakable fashion. And since there is a contingency element in ''being in general'' God cannot even through the sacrifice of Christ have any complete victory over evil. Evil will always have its influence on and in man. Christ cannot defend his own against Satan. When he said that the kingdom of Satan could not prevail against the kingdom of God he had not sufficiently figured with the philosophy of Aristotle. Potentiality can never become exclusively actual.

So it appears that it is only in the Protestant position that the natural man can be confronted with the Christ of the Scriptures as he is in his person and work.

To complete the picture of the work of Christ a word may be said in passing about the doctrine of salvation, of the church, and of the last things.

D. SOTERIOLOGY

We have laid stress upon the organic relation between the offices of Christ. We must now point out that the same organic relationship exists between what Christ did _for_ us and what Christ does _within_ us. In soteriology we deal with the application _to_ us of the redemption Christ has wrought _for_ us. But real redemption has not been fully wrought for us till it is wrought also within us. Sin being what it is, it would be useless to have salvation lie ready to hand unless it were also applied to us. Inasmuch as we are dead in trespasses and sins it would do us no good to have a wonderful life-giving potion laid next to us in our coffin. It would do us good only if someone actually administered the potion to us.

This point is already involved in the fact that Christ must subdue us in order to give us knowledge. But this subduing of us by Christ is done through his Spirit. It is the Spirit who takes the things of Christ and gives them unto us. If Christ is to accomplish his own work fully, the Spirit must do his. For that reason Christ told the disciples it would profit them if he should ascend to heaven. It would only be after his ascent that the Spirit could come and really finish the work that Christ had begun to do while on earth. What Christ did while he was on earth is only a beginning of his work.

It must be noted at this juncture that the Spirit who applies the work of Christ is himself also a member of the ontological Trinity. Unless he were, the work of salvation would not be the work of God alone. The only alternative to this would be that man could at some point take the initiative in the matter of his own salvation. This would imply that the salvation wrought by Christ could be frustrated by man. Suppose that none should accept the salvation offered to them. In that case the whole of Christ's work would be in vain and the eternal creator God would be set at nought by man the creature. If we say that in the case of any sinner the question of salvation is in the last analysis dependent upon man rather than upon God, that is, if we say that man can of himself accept or reject the gospel as he pleases, we have made the eternal God dependent upon man. We have then denied the incommunicable attributes of God. If we refuse to mix the eternal and the temporal at the point of creation and at the point of the incarnation we must also refuse to mix them at the point of salvation.

Here again Romanism occupies a straddling position.

E. ECCLESIOLOGY

"The catholic or universal church, which is invisible, consists of the whole number of the elect, that have been, are, or shall be gathered into one, under Christ the head thereof; and is the spouse, the body, the fulness of him that filleth all in all." This is the Westminster Confession's definition of the church. We need not say much about it for our purposes. It can readily be seen that it is in accord with the preceding statement on soteriology. It contains the same conception of the relation of the eternal to the temporal as is manifest in the doctrine of salvation. In the last analysis it is the eternal that precedes the temporal; it is God who determines the salvation of man; the church, that is, the universal church, is the "whole number of the elect." This does not preclude human responsibility. The confession has spoken of man's responsibility and "free will" in preceding articles. It only brings out clearly that God is absolute, here as elsewhere.

It is this fact of God's absoluteness as expressed in his election of man that gives us courage in preaching and in reasoning with men. Sin being what it is we may be certain that all our preaching and all our reasoning with men will be in vain unless God brings men through it to himself. Men cannot be brought to bay if they have any place to which they can go. Now they do have a place to which they can go if they have the inherent ability to accept or reject the gospel. In that case they need not feel uneasy about rejecting it today because they can accept it tomorrow.

F. ESCHATOLOGY

When we come to the Christian conception of the "last things" we see once more how diametrically the Christian position is set over against that of its opponents. If anywhere, it becomes plain here that in the Christian conception of things God's interpretation of facts precedes the facts. Every Christian who commits his future to God believes that God controls the future. He believes that God has interpreted the future; he believes that the future will come to pass as God has planned it. Prophecy illustrates this point. Belief in the promises of God with respect to our eternal salvation were meaningless unless God controls the future.

Here too we see again that we cannot separate man from the universe around him. Christ spoke of the "regeneration of all things" when he spoke of the end of the world. The promises for the future include a new heaven and a new earth in which righteousness shall dwell. This righteousness includes that the wolf and the lamb shall dwell together. We interpret nature only by the light of the interpretation of God. Then too the time when all this will happen is exclusively in God's hand. If we seek to interpret the "signs of the times" we are to seek to interpret them as God has already interpreted them. We interpret history only by the light of the interpretation of God. The Christian philosophy of nature and the Christian philosophy of history are the diametrical opposites of the non-Christian philosophy of nature and the non-Christian philosophy of history.

CHAPTER II

THE CHRISTIAN PHILOSOPHY OF LIFE

In the first chapter the main concepts of a truly Protestant theology have been placed before us. It might seem then that it would be possible at once to proceed to the defense of these concepts. But this is not so. Before defending Christian theology we must speak of Christianity and its relation to philosophy and to science. Philosophy, as usually defined, deals with a theory of reality, with a theory of knowledge, and with a theory of ethics. That is to say philosophies usually undertake to present a life and world view. They deal not only with that which man can directly experience by means of his senses but also, and ofttimes especially, with the presuppositions of experience. In short, they deal with that which Christian theology speaks of as God. On the other hand Christian theology deals not only with God; it deals also with the "world." It would be quite impossible then to state and vindicate a truly Christian theology without also stating and defending — be it in broad outline only — a Christian philosophy.

Note 1. The Roman Catholic apologists have worked out elaborate arguments to prove that theology and philosophy cover clearly differentiated domains of reality and follow clearly differentiated methods of investigation. Philosophy is said to deal with the domain of the natural reason, and Christianity is said to deal with the domain of faith. Theology, says Jaques Maritain, presupposes certain "fundamental truths of the natural order as an introduction to the faith" (An Introduction to Philosophy, p. 130). On the other hand, "the premises of philosophy are self-supported and are not derived from those of theology" (idem p. 126). At a later point we shall consider this Roman Catholic doctrine of the relation of philosophy to theology more fully. For the moment it may suffice to stress the fact that the history of philosophy tells us of men who have sought to give us a totality view of reality as a whole. It is in relation to them that Christianity must be presented. Christian apologetics must, accordingly, in practice be a vindication of the Christian world and life view as a whole.

Note 2. Calvinistic philosophers, such as D.H.Th. Vollenhoven, Het Calvinisme en de Reformatie der Wysbegeerte, H. Dooyeweerd, De Wysbegeerte der Wetsidee and H.G. Stoker Kristendom en Wetenschap, have also stressed the sharp difference of domain between philosophy and theology. However, they are vigorously opposed to the distinction between reason and faith as made by Roman Catholics. They speak of the frankly religious a priori principles that philosophy must take from the Scripture. Their aim in making a sharp distinction between the domain of philosophy and that of theology is therefore primarily that of showing the variegated richness of the Christian life and world view as a whole. With this aim we are in full agreement. But Christian apologetics must concentrate on the central concepts of the Christian life and world view as a whole. It will stress rather the unity than the discreteness of a truly Christian theology and a truly Christian philosophy. It will make use of the main concepts of a true Christian theology and a true Christian philosophy, combining them for its own purposes.

* * * * * * * * *

What has been said about the relation of theology to philosophy also holds – though less obviously so – with respect to the relation of theology to science. The Christian religion, as outlined in the first chapter, has a definite bearing on the scientific enterprise. Christianity claims to furnish the presuppositions without which a true scientific procedure is unintelligible. Chief of these presuppositions is the idea of God as expressed in the doctrine of the ontological Trinity. In addition there are the doctrines of creation, of providence, and of God's ultimate plan with the universe. Christianity claims that the very aim and method of science require these doctrines as their prerequisites.

It is immediately apparent that many scientists, both of the past and of the present, would think this claim of the Christian religion to be preposterous. Such a claim, these scientists would say, impinges upon the independence of science and makes its efforts meaningless. Is it not of the very essence of a truly scientific attitude that it must be ready to follow out the facts to any conclusion whatsoever? It cannot promise in advance of its effort never to reach any conclusions that shall be out of accord with a theological system that has been constructed on the basis of authority. In reply the Christian apologist claims that on its presuppositions alone is science possible.

Enough has been said to indicate that the Christian religion does make some definite pronouncements about that area of life with which scientists deal. In science no less than in philosophy, as these are currently understood, there are principles of interpretation at work which must of necessity come under the scrutiny of Christian theism. To say the very least, it is possible that the foes of the Christian religion may find in the fields of science and philosophy their springboard from which they take off when they make ready for the attack. Granted then that it is not the business of theologians to be either philosophers or scientists it remains true that Christian theology, and particularly Christian apologetics, has an interest in the fields of philosophy and science. To guard its own integrity a true theology must publish, in broad lines at least, something of the nature of these interests.

The nature of these interests is not difficult to surmise. Using the language of modern diplomacy those who are called upon to vindicate the Christian religion might announce the fact that they cannot be indifferent to the troop movements of any system of philosophy or scientific interpretation that threaten, even if only by implication, the integrity of the main doctrines of Christian theism as these have been set forth. Christian apologetics cannot be indifferent to a system of philosophy or of science which, by its presuppositions and implications, as well as by its open assertions, rejects the doctrine of the ontological Trinity, the doctrine of creation, the doctrine of the fall of man and of his redemption through Christ.

On the other hand Christian theology can well afford to offer lend-lease assistance to such systems of philosophy and science as are consistent with these doctrines.

Here it will at once be asked how a system of philosophy or science can be consonant with the doctrines of religion if these doctrines are given by authority and are all-inclusive in their implications. A solution of the problem as to the relation between theology and philosophy or science might be found, it will be argued, if theology is based on authority and philosophy or science is based on reason. By the employment of reason, science and philosophy may make certain assertions about reality, and by means of revelation theology may make additional assertions about reality. Thus the relation would simply be one of supplementation. Reason would think of itself as a rowboat which can go out into water but which dares not attempt to cross the ocean. Faith in authority would simply take over where reason finds the water too deep. If there would be any control of authority over reason at all, this control would be merely negative. It would be the control of a teacher who merely tells the pupil that he has not found the correct answer to his problem. The child can find the right answer of itself if only it tries again. (This is the Roman Catholic position on the relation of philosophy or science to theology. See e.g., Mahoney – Cartesianism, and Jacques Maritain – Introduction to Philosophy.) Again, a solution of the problem of the relation between theology and philosophy or science may be found, it will be argued, if theology limits its assertions to the realm or dimension of the supernatural and if philosophy or science limits its assertions to the realm or dimension of the natural. Good fences make good neighbors. A true science will want to limit itself in its pronouncements to the description of the facts that it meets. It is of the essence of a true science that it makes no pronouncements about origins and purposes. So too a true philosophy will seek logical relationships between the facts of experience. But the absolutes of religion cannot be reached by means of these logical relationships. Reason therefore does not pretend to speak of God as he exists in himself. Thus both science and philosophy limit themselves to the phenomenal realm and gladly leave the realm of the noumenal to authority and faith. (This is a popular method of approach among orthodox as well as liberal Protestants.)

However, it will be argued further, if one rejects both of these possible solutions and insists that the doctrines of religion deal with the phenomenal as well as with the noumenal while yet they are given by authority, one is bound to seek the destruction both of philosophy and of science. Such a concept of the relation of theology to philosophy and science, it will be contended, is monopolistic and totalitarian.

In reply it must first be admitted that a truly Protestant interpretation of Christianity cannot accept either of the two proffered solutions of the relation of theology to philosophy and science. A truly Protestant view of the assertions of philosophy and science can be self-consciously true only if they are made in the light of the Scripture. Scripture gives definite information of a most fundamental character about all the facts and principles with which philosophy and science deal. For philosophy or science to reject or even to ignore this information is to falsify the picture it gives of the field with which it deals.

This does not imply that philosophy and science must be exclusively dependent upon theology for their basic principles. It implies only that philosophy and science must, as well as theology, turn to Scripture for whatever light it has to offer on general principles and particular facts. In order to do so they may ask the assistance of theology. It is the business of theology to engage in detailed exegesis of Scripture. The philosopher will naturally make use of the fruits of this exegesis. It is also the business of theology to present the truth of Scripture in systematic form. The philosopher and the scientist will naturally also make use of the fruit of this effort. Even so the Christian philosopher and the Christian scientist will be first of all directly dependent upon Scripture itself.

Our conclusion then must be that the defense and vindication of a truly Protestant theology require also a defense and vindication of at least some of the basic principles of a truly Protestant philosophy and science. At this point then a few broad principles of a Protestant philosophy and science must be stated.

Basic to the whole activity of philosophy and science is the idea of the covenant. The idea of the covenant is commonly spoken of in relation to theology alone. It there expresses the idea that in all things man is face to face with God. God is there said to be man's and the world's creator. God is there said to be the one who controls and directs the destiny of all things. But this is tantamount to applying the covenant idea to the philosophic and scientific fields as well as to that of theology. It is difficult to see how the covenant idea can be maintained in theology unless it be also maintained in philosophy and science. To see the face of God everywhere and to do all things, whether we eat or drink or do anything else, to the glory of God, that is the heart of the covenant idea. And that idea is, in the nature of the case, all inclusive. There are two and only two classes of men. There are those who worship and serve the creature and there are those who worship and serve the Creator. There are covenant breakers and there are covenant keepers. In all of men's activities, in their philosophical and scientific enterprises as well as in their worship, men are either covenant keepers or covenant breakers. There are, to be sure, many gradations of self-consciousness with which men fall into either of these two classes. Not all those who are at heart covenant keepers are such self-consciously. So also not all those who are at heart covenant breakers are such self-consciously. It is a part of the task of Christian apologetics to make men self-consciously either covenant keepers or covenant breakers.

If what has just been said on the matter of the covenant be true, it follows that the facts and principles employed by the philosopher and the scientist must first of all be regarded under the aspect of revelation. If man is to react as a covenant being this reaction can only be in response to the revelation of God. As already indicated, the face of God appears in all the facts and principles with which philosophy and science deal. But a complication at once arises from the fact of the twofold form of revelation. There is the revelation in nature and there is the revelation that is given in Scripture. What is the relationship between them? That question must be answered at once. Without an answer to that question the whole philosophic and scientific enterprise is left in the dark.

There are two popular answers to this question. These answers correspond to the answers noted above on the question of the relation between theology and philosophy or science. The Roman Catholic says that philosophy and science make certain assertions about God on the basis of the revelation of God in nature, and adds that theology can make additional assertions about God on the basis of the revelation of God in Scripture and tradition. Many Protestants, unfortunately, also hold to this view (see e.g., Bishop Butler's Analogy and the many books later written in dependence upon it). Others maintain that philosophy and science deal with natural revelation and theology deals with supernatural or biblical revelation. But a truly Protestant conception of the relation between the two forms of revelation cannot accept either of these solutions. There is, to be sure, a measure of truth in both contentions. Philosophy and science deal more especially with man in his relation to the cosmos and theology deals more especially with man in his relation to God. But this is only a matter of degree. And the two forms of revelation cover the dimensions or areas of both.

It is accordingly imperative that we seek to work out in a more truly Protestant fashion the question of the relationship between the two forms of revelation.

The first point of importance to note is that the revelation in Scripture must be made our starting-point. It is only in the light of the Protestant doctrine of Scripture that one can obtain also Protestant doctrine of the revelation of God in nature.

According to the Westminster Confession of Faith, Scripture thinks of man as a covenant being. It tells us that man was originally placed on earth under the terms of the covenant of works. It informs us further that man broke this covenant of works and that God was pleased to carry through his aims with the covenant of works by means of the covenant of grace. Thus Scripture may be said to be the written expression of the provisions of God's covenantal relationship with man.

The Confession further sets forth the Protestant doctrine of Scripture under the four heads of its necessity, its authority, its sufficiency and its perspicuity.

The necessity of Scripture lies in the fact that man has broken the covenant of works. He therefore needs the grace of God. There is no speech or manifestation of grace in nature. (To say that there is, as Butler does in his Analogy, is to defeat the purpose of Protestant apologetics. It is to reduce the very idea of grace in order to make it acceptable to the natural man. The natural man needs grace in its unadulterated form.)

The authority of Scripture is involved in the nature of the revelation that it gives. The central message of the Bible is that of saving grace for man. But saving grace is sovereign grace and God alone knows what it is to give sovereign grace. He alone can speak with authority on it. He is not merely an "expert" on the problem of grace; he is the only one who can dispense it and therefore also the only one who can tell of its nature.

To this necessity and authority there must be added the sufficiency or finality of Scripture. When the sun, of grace has arisen on the horizon of the sinner, the "light of nature" shines only by reflected light. Even when there are some "circumstances concerning the worship of God, the government of the church, common to human actions and societies, which are to be ordered by the light of nature and Christian prudence," they are to be so ordered "according to the general rules of the word, which are always to be observed." The light of Scripture is that superior light which lightens every other light. It is also the final light. God's covenant of grace is his final covenant with man. Its terms must be once for all and finally recorded "against the corruption of the flesh, and the malice of Satan and of the world."

To the necessity, authority and sufficiency of Scripture must finally be added its perspicuity. The distribution of God's grace depends, in the last analysis, upon his sovereign will, but it is mediated always through fully responsible image-bearers of God. God's being is wholly clear to himself and his revelation of himself to sinners is therefore also inherently clear. Not only the learned but also the unlearned "in a due use of the ordinary means" may "attain unto a sufficient understanding" of God's covenant of grace as revealed in Scripture.

With this general view of Scripture in mind, we turn to the question of God's revelation of himself in nature. The first point that calls for reflection here is the fact that it is, according to Scripture itself, the same God who reveals himself in nature and in grace. The God who reveals himself in nature may therefore be described as "infinite in being, glory, blessedness, and perfection, all-sufficient, eternal, unchangeable, incomprehensible, everywhere present, almighty, knowing all things, most wise, most holy, most just, most merciful and gracious, long-suffering, and abundant in goodness and truth." (The Larger Catechism, Q. 7). It is, to be sure, from Scripture rather than from nature that this description of God is drawn. Yet it is this same God, to the extent that he is revealed at all, that is revealed in nature.

Contemplation of this fact seems at once to plunge us into great difficulty. Are we not told that nature reveals nothing of the grace of God? Does not the Confession insist that men cannot be saved except through the knowledge of God, "be they ever so diligent to frame their lives according to the light of nature; and the law of that religion they do profess"? (The Confession of Faith, Chapter X). Saving grace is not manifest in nature; yet it is the God of saving grace who manifests himself by means of nature. How can these two be harmonized?

The answer to this problem must be found in the fact that God is "eternal, incomprehensible, most free, most absolute." Any revelation that God gives of himself is therefore absolutely voluntary. Herein precisely lies the union of the various forms of God's revelation with one another. God's revelation in nature, together with God's revelation in Scripture, form God's one grand scheme of covenant revelation of himself to man. The two forms of revelation must therefore be seen as presupposing and supplementing one another. They are aspects of one general philosophy of history.

1. The Philosophy of History

The philosophy of history that speaks to us from the various chapters of the Confession may be sketched with a few bold strokes. We are told that man could never have had any fruition of God through the revelation that came to him in nature as operating by itself. There was superadded to God's revelation in nature another revelation, a supernaturally communicated positive revelation. Natural revelation, we are virtually told, was from the outset incorporated into the idea of a covenantal relationship of God with man. Thus every dimension of created existence, even the lowest, was enveloped in a form of exhaustively personal relationship between god and man. The "ateleological" no less than the "teleological," the "mechanical" no less than the "spiritual" was covenantal in character.

Being from the outset covenantal in character, the natural revelation of God to man was meant to serve as the playground for the process of differentiation that was to take place in the course of time. The covenant made with Adam was conditional. There would be additional revelation of God in nature after the action of man with respect to the tree of the knowledge of good and evil. This additional revelation would be different from that which had preceded it. And the difference would depend definitely upon a self-conscious covenant act of man with respect to the positively communicated prohibition. We know something of the nature of this new and different revelation of God in nature consequent upon the covenant-breaking act of man. "For the wrath of God is revealed from heaven against all ungodliness and unrighteousness of man" (Rom. 1:18).

Thus God's covenant wrath is revealed in nature after the one all-decisive act of disobedience on the part of the first covenant head. But, together with God's wrath, his grace is also manifest. When the wrath of God made manifest in nature would destroy all men, God makes covenant with Noah that day and night, winter and summer, should continue to the end of time (Gen. 9:11). The rainbow, a natural phenomenon, is but an outstanding illustration of this fact. But all this is in itself incomplete. The covenant with Noah is but a limiting notion in relation to the covenant of saving grace. Through the new and better covenant, man will have true fruition of God. And this fact itself is to be mediated through nature. The prophets, and especially the great Prophet, foretell the future course of nature. The priests of God and most of all the great High Priest of God, hear the answers to their prayers by means of nature. The kings under God, and most of all the Great King of Israel, make nature serve the purposes of redemption. The forces of nature are always at the beck and call of the power of differentiation that works toward redemption and reprobation. It is this idea of a supernatural-natural revelation that comes to such eloquent expression in the Old Testament, and particularly in the Psalms.

Here then is the picture of a well-integrated and unified philosophy of history in which revelation in nature and revelation in Scripture are mutually meaningless without one another and mutually fruitful when taken together.

To bring out the unity and therewith the meaning of this total picture more clearly, we turn now to note the necessity, the authority, the sufficiency and the perspicuity of natural revelation, as these correspond to the necessity, the authority, the sufficiency and the perspicuity of Scripture.

2. The Necessity of Natural Revelation

Speaking first of the necessity of natural revelation we must recall that man was made a covenant personality. Scripture became necessary because of the covenant disobedience of Adam in paradise. This covenant disobedience took place in relation to the supernatural positive revelation that God had given with respect to the tree of the knowledge of good and evil. God chose one tree from among many and "arbitrarily" told man not to eat of it. It is in this connection that we must speak of the necessity of natural revelation. If the tree of the knowledge of good and evil had been naturally different from other trees it could not have served its unique purpose. That the commandment might appear as supernatural the natural had to appear as really natural. The supernatural could not be recognized for what it was unless the natural were also recognized for what it was. There had to be regularity if there was to be a genuine exception.

A further point needs to be noted. God did not give his prohibition so that man might be obedient merely with respect to the tree of the knowledge of good and evil, and that merely at one particular moment of time. He gave the prohibition so that man might learn to be self-consciously obedient in all that he did with respect to all things and throughout all time. Man was meant to glorify God in the "lower" as much as in the "higher" dimensions of life. Man's act with respect to the tree of the knowledge of good and evil was to be but an example to himself of what he should or should not do with respect to all other trees. But for an example to be really an example it must be exceptional. And for the exceptional to be the exceptional there is required that which is regular. Thus we come again to the notion of the necessity of natural revelation as the presupposition of the process of differentiation that history was meant to be.

So far we have spoken of the necessity of natural revelation as it existed before the fall. Carrying on this idea, it follows that we may also speak of the necessity of natural revelation after the fall. Here too the natural or regular has to appear as the presupposition of the exceptional. But the exceptional has now become redemptive. The natural must therefore appear as in need of redemption. After the fall it is not sufficient that the natural should appear as merely regular. The natural must now appear as under the curse of God. God's covenant wrath rests securely and comprehensively upon man and upon all that man has mismanaged. Before the fall the natural as being the merely regular was the presupposition of the supernatural as redemptively covenantal. Grace can be recognized as grace only in contrast to God's curse on nature.

Then too the idea of the supernatural as "example" is again in order here. Grace speaks to man of victory over sin. But the victory this time is to come through the obedience of the second Adam. The regeneration of all things must now be a gift before it can become a task. The natural must therefore by contrast reveal an unalleviated picture of folly and ruin. Nor would the Confession permit us to tone down the rigid character of the absolute contrast between the grace and the curse of God through the idea of "common grace." Common grace is subservient to special or saving grace. As such it helps to bring out the very contrast between this saving grace and the curse of God. When men dream dreams of a paradise regained by means of common grace, they only manifest the "strong delusion" that falls as punishment of God upon those that abuse his natural revelation. Thus the natural as the regular appears as all the more in need of the gift of the grace of God.

Yet the gift is in order to the task. The example is also meant to be a sample. Christ walks indeed a cosmic road. Far as the curse is found, so far his grace is given. The biblical miracles of healing point to the regeneration of all things. The healed souls of men require and will eventually receive healed bodies and a healed environment. Thus there is unity of concept for those who live by the scriptural promise of comprehensive though not universal redemption. While they actually expect Christ to return visibly on the clouds of heaven, they thank God for every sunny day. They even thank God for his restraining and supporting general grace by means of which the unbeliever helps to display the majesty and power of

God. To the believer the natural or regular with all its complexity always appears as the playground for the process of differentiation which leads ever onward to the fulness of the glory of God.

3. The Authority of Natural Revelation

So far we have found that the Confession's conception of the necessity of Scripture requires a corresponding conception of the necessity of revelation in nature. It is not surprising then, that the Confession's notion of the authority of Scripture requires a corresponding notion of the authority of revelation in nature. Here too it is well that we begin by studying the situation as it obtained before the entrance of sin.

In paradise, God communicated directly and positively with man in regard to the tree of life. This revelation was authoritative. Its whole content was that of a command requiring implicit obedience. This supernatural revelation was something exceptional. To be recognized for what it was in its exceptionality, a contrast was required between it and God's regular way of communication with man. Ordinarily man had to use his God-given powers of investigation to discover the workings of the processes of nature. Again, the voice of authority as it came to man in this exceptional manner was to be but illustrative of the fact that, in and through the things of nature, there spoke the self-same voice of God's command. Man was given permission by means of the direct authority to control and subdue the powers of nature. As a hunter bears upon his back in clearly visible manner the number of his hunting license, so Adam bore indelibly upon his mind the divine right of dealing with nature. And the divine right was at the same time the divine obligation. The mark of God's ownership was from the beginning writ large upon all the facts of the universe. Man was to cultivate the garden of the Lord and gladly pay tribute to the Lord of the manor.

Man's scientific procedure was accordingly to be marked by the attitude of obedience to God. He was to realize that he would find death in nature everywhere if he manipulated it otherwise than as being the direct bearer of the behests of God. The rational creature of God must naturally live by authority in all the activities of his personality. All these activities are inherently covenantal activities either of obedience or of disobedience. Man was created as an analogue of God; his thinking, his willing, and his doing is therefore properly conceived as at every point analogical to the thinking, willing and doing of God. It is only after refusing to be analogous to God that man can think of setting a contrast between the attitude of reason to one type of revelation and the attitude of faith to another type of revelation.

By the idea of revelation, then, we are to mean not merely what comes to man through the facts surrounding him in his environment, but also that which comes to him by means of his own constitution as a covenant personality. The revelation that comes to man by way of his own rational and moral nature is no less objective to him than that which comes to him through the voice of trees and animals. Man's own psychological activity is no less revelational than the laws of physics about him. All created reality is inherently revelational of the nature and will of God. Even man's ethical reaction to God's revelation is still revelational. And as revelational of God, it is authoritative. The meaning of the Confession's doctrine of the authority of Scripture does not become clear to us till we see it against the background of the original and basically authoritative character of God's revelation in nature. Scripture speaks authoritatively to such as must naturally live by authority. God speaks with authority wherever and whenever he speaks.

At this point a word may be said about the revelation of God through conscience and its relation to Scripture. Conscience is man's consciousness speaking on matters of directly moral import. Every act of man's consciousness is moral in the most comprehensive sense of that term. Yet there is a difference between questions of right and wrong in a restricted sense and general questions of interpretation. Now if man's whole consciousness was originally created perfect, and as such authoritatively expressive of the will of God, that same consciousness is still revelational and authoritative after the entrance of sin to the extent that its voice is still the voice of God. The sinner's efforts, so far as they are done self-consciously from his point of view, seek to destroy or bury the voice of God that comes to him through nature, which includes his own consciousness. But this effort cannot be wholly successful at any point in history. The most depraved of men cannot wholly escape the voice of God. Their greatest wickedness is meaningless except upon the assumption that they have sinned against the authority of God. Thoughts and deeds of utmost perversity are themselves revelational; revelational, that is, in their very abnormality. The natural man accuses or else excuses himself only because his own utterly depraved consciousness continues to point back to the original natural state of affairs. The prodigal son can never forget the father's voice. It is the albatross forever about his neck.

4. The Sufficiency of Natural Revelation

Proceeding now to speak of the sufficiency of natural revelation as corresponding to the sufficiency of Scripture, we recall that revelation in nature was never meant to function by itself. It was from the beginning insufficient without its supernatural concomitant. It was inherently a limiting notion. It was but the presupposition of historical action on the part of man as covenant personality with respect to supernaturally conveyed communication. But for that specific purpose it was wholly sufficient. It was historically sufficient.

After the fall of man natural revelation is still historically sufficient. It is sufficient for such as have in Adam brought the curse of God upon nature. It is sufficient to render them without excuse. Those who are in prison and cannot clearly see the light of the sun receive their due inasmuch as they have first abused that light. If nature groans in pain and travail because of man's abuse of it, this very fact — that is, the very curse of God on nature — should be instrumental anew in making men accuse or excuse themselves. Nature as it were yearns to be released from its imprisonment in order once more to be united to her Lord in fruitful union. When nature is abused by man it cries out to its creator for vengeance and through it, for redemption.

It was in the mother promise that God gave the answer to nature's cry (Gen. 3:15). In this promise there was a two-fold aspect. There was first the aspect of vengeance. He that should come was to bruise the head of the serpent, the one that led men in setting up nature as independent of the supernatural revelation of God. Thus nature was once more to be given the opportunity of serving as the proper field of exercise for the direct supernatural communication of God to man. But this time this service came at a more advanced point in history. Nature was now the bearer of God's curse as well as of his general mercy. The "good," that is, the believers, are, generally, hedged about by God. Yet they must not expect that always and in every respect this will be the case. They must learn to say with Job, be it after much trial, "Though he slay me, yet will I trust in him" (Job 13:15). The "evil," that is, the unbelievers, will generally be rewarded with the natural consequences of their deeds. But this too is not always and without qualification the case. The wicked sometimes prosper. Nature only shows tendencies. And tendencies point forward to the time when tendencies shall have become the rules without the exception. The tendency itself is meaningless without the certainty of the climax. The present regularity of nature is therefore once again to be looked upon as a limiting notion. At every stage in history God's revelation in nature is sufficient for the purpose it was meant to serve, that of being the playground for the process of differentiation between those who would and those who would not serve God.

5. The Perspicuity of Natural Revelation

Finally we turn to the perspicuity of nature which corresponds to the perspicuity of Scripture. We have stressed the fact that God's revelation in nature was from the outset of history meant to be taken conjointly with God's supernatural communication. This might seem to indicate that natural revelation is not inherently perspicuous. Then too it has been pointed out that back of both kinds of revelation is the incomprehensible God. And this fact again might, on first glance, seem to militate strongly against the claim that nature clearly reveals God. Yet these very facts themselves are the best guarantee of the genuine perspicuity of natural revelation. The perspicuity of God's revelation in nature depends for its very meaning upon the fact that it is an aspect of the total and totally voluntary revelation of a God who is self-contained. God's incomprehensibility to man is due to the fact that he is exhaustively comprehensible to himself. God is light and in him is no darkness at all. As such he cannot deny himself. This God naturally has an all-comprehensive plan for the created universe. He has planned all the relationships between all the aspects of created being. He has planned the end from the beginning. All created reality therefore actually displays this plan. It is, in consequence, inherently rational.

It is quite true, of course, that created man is unable to penetrate to the very bottom of this inherently clear revelation. But this does not mean that on this account the revelation of God is not clear, even for him. Created man may see clearly what is revealed clearly even if he cannot see exhaustively. Man does not need to know exhaustively in order to know truly and certainly. When on the created level of existence man thinks God's thoughts after him, that is, when man thinks in self-conscious submission to the voluntary revelation of the self-sufficient God, he has therewith the only possible ground of certainty for his knowledge. When man thinks thus he thinks as a covenant creature would wish to think. That is to say, man normally thinks in analogical fashion. He realizes that God's thoughts are self-contained. He knows that his own interpretation of nature must therefore be a re-interpretation of what is already fully interpreted by God.

The concept of analogical thinking is of especial significance here. Soon we shall meet with a notion of analogy that is based upon the very denial of the concept of the incomprehensible God. It is therefore of the utmost import that the Confession's concept of analogical thinking be seen to be the direct implication of its doctrine of God.

One further point must be noted here. We have seen that since the fall of man God's curse rests upon nature. This has brought great complexity into the picture. All this, however, in no wise detracts from the historical and objective perspicuity of nature. Nature can and does reveal nothing but the one comprehensive plan of God. The psalmist does not say that the heavens possibly or probably declare the glory of God. Nor does the apostle assert that the wrath of God is probably revealed from heaven against all ungodliness and unrighteousness of men. Scripture takes the clarity of God's revelation for granted at every stage of human history. Even when man, as it were, takes out his own eyes, this act itself turns revelational in his wicked hands, testifying to him that his sin is a sin against the light that lighteth every man coming into the world. Even to the very bottom of the most complex historical situations, involving sin and all its consequences, God's revelation shines with unmistakable clarity. "If I make my bed in hell, behold thou art there" (Psalm 139:8). Creatures have no private chambers.

Both the perspicuity of Scripture and the perspicuity of natural revelation, then, may be said to have their foundation in the doctrine of the God who "hideth himself," whose thoughts are higher than man's thoughts and whose ways are higher than man's ways. There is no discrepancy between the idea of mystery and that of perspicuity with respect either to revelation in Scripture or to revelation in nature. On the contrary the two ideas are involved in one another. The central unifying concept of the entire Confession is the doctrine of God and his one unified comprehensive plan for the world. The contention consequently is that at no point is there any excuse for man's not seeing all things as happening according to this plan.

In considering man's acceptance of natural revelation, we again take our clue from the Confession and what it says about the acceptance of Scripture. Its teaching on man's acceptance of scriptural revelation is in accord with its teachings on the necessity, authority, sufficiency and perspicuity of Scripture. The Scriptures as the finished product of God's supernatural and saving revelation to man have their own evidence in themselves. The God who speaks in Scripture cannot refer to anything that is not already authoritatively revelational of himself for the evidence of his own existence. There is no thing that does not exist by his creation. All things take their meaning from him. Every witness to him is a "prejudiced" witness. For any fact to be a fact at all, it must be a revelational fact.

It is accordingly no easier for sinners to accept God's revelation in nature than to accept God's revelation in Scripture. They are no more ready of themselves to do the one than to do the other. From the point of view of the sinner, theism is as objectionable as is Christianity. Theism that is worthy of the name is Christian theism. Christ said that no man can come to the Father but by him. No one can become a theist unless he becomes a Christian. Any god that is not the Father of our Lord Jesus Christ is not God but an idol.

It is therefore the Holy Spirit bearing witness by and with the Word in our hearts that alone effects the required Copernican revolution and makes us both Christians and theists. Before the fall, man also needed the witness of the Holy Spirit. Even then the third person of the Holy Trinity was operative in and through the naturally revelational consciousness of man so that it might react fittingly and properly to the words of God's creation. But then that operation was so natural that man himself needed not at all or scarcely to be aware of its existence. When man fell, he denied the naturally revelatory character of every fact including that of his own consciousness. He assumed that he was autonomous; he assumed that his consciousness was not revelational of God but only of himself. He assumed himself to be non-created. He assumed that the work of interpretation, as by the force of his natural powers he was engaged in it, was an original instead of a derivative procedure. He would not think God's thoughts after him; he would instead think only his own original thoughts.

Now if anything is obvious from Scripture it is that man is not regarded as a proper judge of God's revelation to him. Man is said or assumed from the first page to the last to be a creature of God. God's consciousness is therefore taken to be naturally original as man's is naturally derivative. Man's natural attitude in all self-conscious activities was therefore meant to be that of obedience. It is to this deeper depth, deeper than the sinner's consciousness can ever reach by itself, that Scripture appeals when it says: "Come let us reason together." It appeals to covenant-breakers and argues

with them about the unreasonableness of covenant-breaking. And it is only
when the Holy Spirit gives man a new heart that he will accept the evidence
of Scripture about itself and about nature for what it really is. The Holy
Spirit's regenerating power enables man to place all things in true perspective.

Man the sinner, as Calvin puts it, through the testimony of the Spirit
receives a new power of sight by which he can appreciate the new light that
has been given in Scripture. The new light and the new power of sight imply
one another. The one is fruitless for salvation without the other. It is by
grace, then, by the gift of the Holy Spirit alone, that sinners are able to observe the fact that all nature, including even their own negative attitude toward God, is revelational of God, the God of Scripture. The wrath of God
is revealed, Paul says, on all those who keep down the truth. Man's sinful
nature has become his second nature. This sinful nature of man must now
be included in nature as a whole. And through it God is revealed. He is
revealed as the just one, as the one who hates iniquity and punishes it. Yet
he must also be seen as the one who does not yet punish to the full degree
of their ill dessert the wicked deeds of sinful men.

All this is simply to say that one must be a believing Christian to
study nature in the proper frame of mind and with the proper procedure. It is
only the Christian consciousness that is ready and willing to regard all nature, including man's own interpretative reactions, as revelational of God.
But this very fact requires that the Christian consciousness make a sharp
distinction between what is revelational in this broad and basic sense and
what is revelational in the restricted sense. When man had not sinned, he
was naturally anxious constantly to seek contact with the supernatural positive revelation of God. But it is a quite different matter when we think of
the redeemed sinner. He is restored to the right relationship. But he is
restored in principle only. There is a drag upon him. His "old man" wants
him to interpret nature apart from the supernatural revelation in which he
operates. The only safeguard he has against this historical drag is to test
his interpretations constantly by the principles of the written Word. And if
theology succeeds in bringing forth ever more clearly the depth of the riches
of the biblical revelation of God in Scripture, the Christian philosopher or
scientist will be glad to make use of this clearer and fuller interpretation
in order that his own interpretation of nature may be all the fuller and clearer too, and thus more truly revelational of God. No subordination of philosophy or science to theology is intended here. The theologian is simply a
specialist in the field of biblical interpretation taken in the more restricted
sense. The philosopher is directly subject to the Bible and must in the last
analysis rest upon his own interpretation of the Word. But he may accept
the help of those who are more constantly and more exclusively engaged in
biblical study than he himself can be.

CHAPTER III

THE POINT OF CONTACT

In the two preceding chapters it has been our chief concern to set forth the salient features of the Christian life and world view. The Christian life and world view, it was argued, presents itself as an <u>absolutely comprehensive</u> interpretation of human experience. The Christian life and world view, it was further argued, presents itself as the <u>only true</u> interpretation of human experience.

From the consideration of the content and claim of Christianity as a life and world view our task now calls us to a consideration of its defense. We have seen, in broad outline, what Christianity is; the question now is as to how it is to be vindicated as exclusively true.

In what follows it will be impossible to deal with this question in detail. Our concern will be with general principles only.

The first matter to be considered will be that of the point of contact. Is there something on which believers in Christianity and disbelievers agree? Is there an area known by both from which, as a starting point, we may go on to that which is known to believers but unknown to unbelievers? And is there a common method of knowing this "known area" which need only to be applied to that which the unbeliever does not know in order to convince him of its existence and its truth? It will not do to assume at the outset that these questions must be answered in the affirmative. For the <u>knower</u> himself needs interpretation as well as the things he knows. The human mind, it is now commonly recognized, as the knowing subject, makes its contribution to the knowledge it obtains. It will be quite impossible then to find a common area of knowledge between believers and unbelievers unless there is agreement between them as to the nature of man himself. But there is no such agreement. In his recent work An Essay on Man, Ernest Cassirer traces the various theories of man that have been offered by philosophers in the course of the ages. The modern theory of man, Cassirer asserts, has lost its intellectual center. "He acquired instead a complete anarchy of thought. Even in former times to be sure there was a great discrepancy of opinions and theories relating to this problem. But there remained at least a general orientation, a frame of reference, to which all individual differences might be referred. Metaphysics, theology, mathematics, and biology successively assumed the guidance for thought on the problem of man and determined the line of investigation. The real crisis of this problem manifested itself when such a central power capable of directing all individual efforts ceased to exist. The paramount importance of the problem was still felt in all the different branches of knowledge and inquiry. But an established authority to which one might appeal no longer existed. Theologians, scientists, politicians, sociologists, biologists, psychologists, ethnologists, economists, all approached the problem from their own viewpoints. To combine or unify all these particular aspects and perspectives was impossible. And even within the special fields there was no generally accepted scientific principle. The personal factor became more and more prevalent, and the temperament of the individual writer tended to play a decisive role. Trahit sua quemque voluptae; every author seems in the last count to be led by his own conception and evaluation of human life'' (Op. cit., p. 21).

The confusion of modern anthropology as here portrayed by Cassirer is in itself distressing enough. But one point, at least, is clear. The conception of man as entertained by modern thought in general cannot be assumed to be the same as that set forth in Scripture. It is therefore imperative that the Christian apologist be alert to the fact that the average person to whom he must present the Christian religion for acceptance is a quite different sort of being than he himself thinks he is. A good doctor will not prescribe medicines according to the diagnosis that his patient has made of himself. The patient may think that he needs nothing more than a bottle of medicine while the doctor knows that an immediate operation is required.

Christianity then must present itself as the light that makes the facts of human experience, and above all the nature of man himself, to appear for what they really are. Christianity is the source from which both life and light derive for men.

Roman Catholicism on the Starting Point

It is of the utmost importance to stress the point just made. If a Protestant finds it necessary to dispute with the Roman Catholic on the nature of Christianity itself he will find it equally necessary to dispute with him on the problem of the point of contact. A Protestant theology requires a Protestant apologetic.

Rome's Doctrine

The difference between a Protestant and a Roman Catholic conception of the point of contact will naturally have to be formulated in a way similar to that in which we state the difference between a Protestant and a Roman Catholic theology. There are two ways of stating this difference. One very common way is to indicate first an area of doctrine that the two types of theology have in common, in order afterwards to enumerate the differences between them. This is the course followed in B.B.Warfield's justly famous little book, The Plan of Salvation. Between those holding to a plan of salvation, says Warfield, there are those who think of this plan along naturalist and there are others who think of this plan along supernaturalist lines. As against the Pelagians who hold to a naturalist view ''the entire organized Church — Orthodox Greek, Roman Catholic, Latin, and Protestantism in all its great historical forms, Lutheran and Reformed, Calvinistic and Wes-

39

leyan – bears its consentient, firm and emphatic testimony to the supernaturalistic conception of salvation'' (Philadelphia 1918, p. 17).

Continuing from this point Warfield then divides the supernaturalists into sacerdotalists and evangelicals. The issue between them concerns ''the immediacy of the saving operations of God. '' The church of Rome, holding the sacerdotal point of view, teaches that ''grace is communicated by and through the ministrations of the church, otherwise not'' (p. 18). On the other hand, evangelicalism ''seeking to conserve what it conceives to be the only consistent supernaturalism, sweeps away every intermediary between the soul and its God, and leaves the soul dependent for its salvation of God alone, operating upon it by his immediate grace'' (p. 19). Now Protestantism and Evangelicalism are ''coterminous, if not exactly synonymous designations'' (p. 20).

At this point Warfield goes on to mark the main variations within Protestantism. ''Among Protestants or evangelicals there are those who hold to a universalistic and there are those who hold to a particularistic conception of the plan of salvation. All evangelicals agree that all the power exerted in saving the soul is from God and that this saving power is exerted immediately upon the soul. But they differ as to whether God exerts this saving power equally, or at least indiscriminately, upon all men, be they actually saved or not, or rather only upon particular men, namely upon those who are actually saved'' (p. 22). Signalizing the difference between universalistic and particularistic evangelicals again, Warfield uses these words, ''The precise issue which divides the universalists and the particularists is, accordingly, just whether the saving grace of God, in which alone is salvation, actually saves'' (p. 24).

It is not germane to our purpose to follow Warfield further as he differentiates once more between various forms of particularists. The ''differences of large moment'' (p. 24) are now before us. Warfield defends particularism or Calvinism. And it has become customary to use the term evangelical with reference to non-Calvinistic Protestants.

What interests us now is the fact that, though beginning from the common denominator point of view, Warfield is compelled, each time he signalizes a new difference, to indicate that it is made in the interest of consistency. Protestants are Protestants in the interest of being more consistently supernaturalist than are the Roman Catholics. Calvinists are particularists in the interest of being more consistently evangelical than are the other Protestants. Calvinists aim at holding a position, according to Warfield, that shall be ''uncolored by intruding elements from without'' (p. 21). Accordingly the several conceptions of salvation ''do not stand simply side by side as varying conceptions of that plan, each making its appeal in opposition to all the rest. They are related to one another rather as a progressive series of corrections of a primal error, attaining ever more and more consistency in the embodiment of the one fundamental idea of salvation'' (p. 31).

It appears then that Warfield himself really suggests a better way of expressing such differences as obtain between Romanism and Protestantism, or between universalistic and particularistic Protestantism than he has himself employed. That better way is pointed out by Professor John Murray when he says, "It would appear, therefore, that the truer, more effective and, on all accounts, more secure defense of Christianity and exposition of its essential content is not to take our starting point from those terms that will express the essential creedal confession of some of its most widely known historical deformations but rather from those terms that most fully express and give character to that redemptive religion which Christianity is. In other words, Christianity cannot receive proper understanding or its exposition proper orientation unless it is viewed as that which issues from, and is consummated in the accomplishment of the covenantal counsel and purpose of Father, Son and Holy Spirit" (The Westminster Theological Journal, Vol. IX, Number 1, p. 90). We are not to define the essence of Christianity in terms of its lowest but rather in terms of its highest forms. Calvinism is "Christianity come to its own." Beginning from Calvinism we should descend to universalistic Protestantism and thence to Romanism as deviations from the true view of Christianity.

It is Romanism with which we are now primarily concerned. Accordingly Romanism should be regarded as a deformation of Christianity, in fact as its lowest deformation. And this deformation expresses itself not merely at some but at every point of doctrine. The differences between Protestantism and Romanism are not adequately indicated if we say that Luther restored to the church the true doctrines of the Bible, of justification by faith and of the priesthood of all believers. The difference is rather that Protestantism is more consistently and Rome is less consistently Christian at every point of doctrine. It could not well be otherwise. Having inconsistency at one point of doctrine is bound to result in inconsistency at all points of doctrine. Rome has been consistently inconsistent in the confusion of non-Christian with Christian elements of teaching along the entire gamut of doctrinal expression.

The bearing of all this on the question of starting point may now be briefly suggested. In the question of starting point it is all-important that we have a truly Christian doctrine of man. But this Rome does not have. Without going into details it may be asserted that Rome has a defective doctrine (a) with respect to the nature of man as he was created and (b) with respect to the effect of the entrance of sin upon the nature of man. "The important point of difference is," says Charles Hodge, "that Protestants hold that original righteousness, so far as it consisted in the moral excellence of Adam, was natural, while the Romanists maintain that it was supernatural. According to their theory, God created man soul and body. These two constituents of his nature are naturally in conflict. To preserve the harmony between them, and the due subjection of the flesh to the spirit, God gave man the supernatural gift of original righteousness. It was this gift that man lost by his fall; so that since the apostacy he is in the state in which Adam was before he was invested with this supernatural endowment. In opposition to this doctrine, Protestants maintain that original righteousness was concreated and natural'' (Systematic Theology, Vol. II, p. 103). The objections to this view, as Hodge enumerates them are, (1) ''That it supposes a degrading view of the original constitution of our nature. According to this doctrine the seeds of evil were implanted in the nature of man as it came from the hands of God. It was disordered or diseased, there was about it what Bellarmin calls a morbus or languor, which needed a remedy ...'' (2) ''This doctrine as to original righteousness arose out of the Semi-Pelagianism of the Church of Rome, and was designed to sustain it''(Op.cit., p. 105).

Suppose then that a Romanist approaches an unbeliever and asks him to accept Christianity. The unbeliever, in his eyes, is merely such an one as has lost original righteousness. The image of God in him which, according to Romanism consists as Hodge says, ''only of the rational, and especially the voluntary nature of man, or the freedom of the will'' (p. 103), is thought of as still intact. That is to say, the unbeliever is, perhaps barring extremes, correct in what he himself thinks of the powers of his intellect and will. There is not necessarily any sin involved in what the unbeliever, or natural man, does by way of exercising his capacities for knowledge and action. On this view the natural man does not need the light of Christianity to enable him to understand the world and himself aright. He does not need the revelation of Scripture or the illumination of the Holy Spirit in order that by means of them he may learn what his own true nature is.

Christianity therefore needs, on this basis, to be presented to the natural man as something that is merely information additional to what he already possesses. The knowledge of Christianity is to be related to the knowledge derived from the exercise of man's powers of reason and observation in a way similar to that in which at the beginning original righteousness was added to the image of God in man.

But without the light of Christianity it is as little possible for man to have the correct view about himself and the world as it is to have the true view about God. On account of the fact of sin man is blind with respect to the truth wherever the truth appears. And truth is one. Man cannot truly know himself unless he truly knows God. Not recognizing the fact of the fall, the philosophers, says Calvin, throw everything into confusion. They do not reckon with the fact that ''at first every part of the soul was formed to rectitude'' but that after the fall man is equally corrupt in all aspects of his being'' (Institutes I, 5:7). ''They tell us,'' says Calvin, ''there is great repugnance between the organic movements and the rational part of the soul. As if reason also were not at variance with herself, and her counsels sometimes conflicting with each other like hostile armies. But since this disorder results from the deprivation of nature, it is erroneous to infer that there are two souls, because the faculties do not accord harmoniously as they ought'' (I, 15:6).

42

It appears then that there is a fundamental difference of opinion between Romanism and Calvin on the origin and nature of the "disturbance" in human nature. The view of Rome is essentially the same as that of the Greek philosophers: in particular, that of Aristotle. According to this view the disturbance is endemic to human nature because man is made up, in part, of non-rational elements. To the extent that man consists of intellect he does not and cannot sin. The "disturbance" in man's make-up is not due primarily to any fault of his own. It is basically due to "God" who made him. On the other hand, according to Calvin, there is no "disturbance" in the nature of man as he comes forth from the hands of God. The "disturbance" has come in as the result of sin. Accordingly every one of fallen man's functions operates wrongly. The set of the whole human personality has changed. The intellect of fallen man may, as such, be keen enough. It can therefore formally understand the Christian position. It may be compared to a buzz-saw that is sharp and shining, ready to cut the boards that come to it. Let us say that a carpenter wishes to cut fifty boards for the purpose of laying the floor of a house. He has marked his boards. He has set his saw. He begins at one end of the mark on the board. But he does not know that his seven year old son has tampered with the saw and changed its set. The result is that every board he saws is cut slantwise and thus unusable because too short except at the point where the saw first made its contact with the wood. As long as the set of the saw is not changed the result will always be the same. So also whenever the teachings of Christianity are presented to the natural man they will be cut according to the set of sinful human personality. The keener the intellect the more consistently will the truths of Christianity be cut according to an exclusively immanentistic pattern. The result is that however much they may formally understand the truth of Christianity, men still worship "the dream and figment of their own heart" (Institutes, I, 4:1). They have what Hodge calls "mere cognition," but no true knowledge of God.

Still further as the "philosophers" and Calvin differ on the source and nature of the "disturbance" in human nature so they also differ on the remedy to be employed for the removal of that disturbance. According to the philosophers man does not need supernatural help for the removal of the disturbance within his being. According to the Greek view, so largely followed by Rome, man's intellect has within itself the proper set. The fall has not disturbed the set of the saw and therefore there is no need of the supernatural power of the Holy Spirit to reset it. The nature of the intellect and its activity is almost unaffected by what happens to man in the course of history.

In opposition to this view, Hodge, following the lead of Calvin, stresses the fact that the whole set of sinful man needs to be renewed by the power of the Holy Spirit. The natural man must be "renewed in knowledge after the image of him that created him" (Col. 3:10). "New man ($\nu \acute{e} o \nu$)" says Hodge, in exposition of St. Paul, "agreeably to the ordinary distinction between $\nu \acute{e} o \nu$ and $\kappa \alpha \iota \nu \acute{o} s$ means recent, newly made, as opposed to ($\pi \alpha \lambda \alpha \iota o s$) old. The moral quality or excellence of this recently formed man is expressed in

the word $\overset{,}{\alpha}\nu\alpha\kappa\alpha\iota\nu o\acute{\upsilon}\mu\epsilon\nu o\nu$ as in Scriptural usage what is $\kappa\alpha\iota\nu o\acute{s}$, is
pure. This renovation is said to be $\epsilon\iota s$ $\overset{,}{\epsilon}\pi\iota\gamma\nu\omega\sigma\iota\nu$ not in knowledge, much
less by knowledge, but unto knowledge, so that he knows. Knowledge is the
effect of the renovation spoken of'' (Systematic Theology, Vol. II, p. 99). A
little further Hodge adds: ''The knowledge here intended is not mere cognition. It is full, accurate, living, or practical knowledge; such knowledge as
is eternal life, so that this word here includes what in Ephesians 4:24 is expressed by righteousness and holiness'' (ibid).

Hodge also exegetes Ephesians 4:24, ''Put on the new man, which after
God is created in righteousness and true holiness.'' ''These words,'' says
Hodge, ''when used in combination are intended to be exhaustive: i. e., to include all moral excellence. Either term may be used in this comprehensive
sense, but, when distinguished, $\delta\iota\kappa\alpha\iota o\sigma\acute{\upsilon}\nu\eta$ means rectitude, the being
and doing right, what justice demands; $\overset{,}{o}\sigma\iota o\acute{\tau}\eta s$ purity, holiness, the state
of mind produced when the soul is full of God. Instead of true holiness, the
words of the Apostle should be rendered 'righteousness and holiness of the
truth'; that is, the righteousness and holiness which are the effects or mani-
festations of the truth. By truth here as opposed to the deceit ($\overset{,}{\alpha}\pi\alpha\acute{\tau}\eta$)
mentioned in the twenty-second verse, is meant what in Colossians 3:10 is
called knowledge. It is the divine light in the understanding, of which the
Spirit of truth is the author, and from which, as their proximate cause, all
right affections and holy acts proceed'' (Idem, p. 101). Repeatedly Hodge
stresses the fact that according to Scripture the natural man is incapable of
himself to understand and accept the truth of Christianity. ''The natural man,
man as he is by nature, is destitute of the life of God, i. e., of spiritual life.
His understanding is darkness, so that he does not know or receive the things
of God. He is not susceptible of impression from the realities of the spiritual
world. He is as insensible to them as a dead man to the things of this world''
(Idem, p. 244). In discussing regeneration Hodge asserts, ''The Bible makes
eternal life to consist in knowledge; sinfulness is blindness; or darkness; the
transition from a state of sin to a state of holiness is a translation from darkness into light; men are said to be renewed unto knowledge, i. e., knowledge
is the effect of regeneration, conversion is said to be effected by the revelation of Christ; the rejection of Him as the Son of God and Saviour of men is
referred to the fact that the eyes of those who believe not are blinded by the
god of this world'' (Vol. III, p. 16). Or again, ''The heart in Scripture is
that which thinks, feels, wills, and acts. It is the soul, the self. A new heart
is, therefore, a new self, a new man. It implies a change of the whole character. It is a new nature. Out of the heart proceed all conscious, voluntary,
moral exercises. A change of heart, therefore, is a change which precedes
these exercises and determines their character'' (Idem, p. 35). ''According
to the evangelical doctrine the whole soul is the subject of regeneration. It
is neither the intellect to the exclusion of the feelings, nor the feelings to the
exclusion of the intellect; nor is it the will alone, either in its wider or in its
more limited sense, that is the subject of the change in question...'' ''Regeneration secures right knowledge as well as right feeling; and right feeling

is not the effect of right knowledge, nor is right knowledge the effect of right feeling. The two are the inseparable effects of a work which affects the whole soul" (Idem, p. 36).

We conclude then that it is natural and consistent for Roman Catholic apologetics to seek its point of contact with the unbeliever in a "common area" of knowledge. Roman Catholic theology agrees with the essential contention of those it seeks to win to the Christian faith that man's consciousness of himself and of the objects of the world is intelligible without reference to God.

But herein precisely lies the fundamental point of difference between Romanism and Protestantism. According to the principle of Protestantism, man's consciousness of self and of objects presuppose for their intelligibility the consciousness of God. In asserting this we are not thinking of psychological and temporal priority. We are thinking only of the question as to what is the final reference point in interpretation. The Protestant principle finds this in the self-contained ontological Trinity. By his counsel the triune God controls whatsoever comes to pass. If then the human consciousness must, in the nature of the case, always be the proximate starting point, it remains true that God is always the most basic and therefore the ultimate or final reference point in human interpretation.

This is, in the last analysis, the question as to what are one's ultimate presuppositions. When man became a sinner he made of himself instead of God the ultimate or final reference point. And it is precisely this presupposition, as it controls without exception all forms of non-Christian philosophy, that must be brought into question. If this presupposition is left unquestioned in any field all the facts and arguments presented to the unbeliever will be made over by him according to his pattern. The sinner has cemented colored glasses to his eyes which he cannot remove. And all is yellow to the jaundiced eye. There can be no intelligible reasoning unless those who reason together understand what they mean by their words.

In not challenging this basic presupposition with respect to himself as the final reference point in predication the natural man may accept the "theistic proofs" as fully valid. He may construct such proofs. He has constructed such proofs. But the God whose existence he proves to himself in this way is always a God who is something other than the self-contained ontological Trinity of Scripture. But the Roman Catholic apologete does not want to prove the existence of this sort of God. He wants to prove the existence of such a God as will leave intact the autonomy of man to at least some extent. Rome's theology does not want a God whose counsel controls whatsoever comes to pass.

It is natural then that Rome's view of the point of contact with the unbeliever is what it is.

Non-Calvinistic Protestantism

We have spoken of the basic difference between Romanism and Protestantism on this question of the point of contact. But not all Protestantism has been fully true to the Protestant principle. Warfield has pointed this out admirably in the book discussed. It was only in Calvinism that the Protestant principle that salvation is of God alone has come to its consistent expression. Non-Calvinistic Protestants, frequently spoken of as Evangelicals, have conceived of "the operations of God looking to salvation universalistically" in order to leave room for an ultimate decision on the part of the individual human being (Warfield, op. cit., p. 111). God, as it were, through Christ deposits a large sum of money in a bank and announces this fact in the daily papers, offering to each one who comes sufficient for all his needs. It is then, in the last analysis, up to the individual whether he wants to be and remain in the class of those who live by the generosity of this bank. God approaches man by means of universals. There are differences among evangelicals, but, in the last analysis, these differences are merely as to whether God approaches the individuals by means of a wider or a narrower species. The final issue is always left up to the individual. "Particularism in the process of salvation becomes thus the mark of Calvinism" (Warfield, op. cit., p. 111). Warfield speaks therefore of Calvinism as being the only form of Protestantism "uncolored by intruding elements from without." God's action is the ultimate source of all determinate being.

For our purposes then the point of importance is that Evangelicalism has retained something of Roman Catholicism both in its view of man and in its view of God. Like Romanism, Evangelicalism thinks of human self-consciousness and consciousness of objects as to some extent intelligible without the consciousness of God. It is to be expected that Evangelicalism will be in agreement with Rome on the question of the point of contact. Both forms of theology are colored by elements of an underlying naturalism. Both are therefore unwilling to challenge the natural man's basic presupposition with respect to himself as the ultimate reference point in interpretation. Both are unwilling to prove the existence of such a God as controls whatsoever comes to pass.

The great textbook of Evangelical apologetics is Bishop Butler's famous Analogy. It is not our purpose here to deal with its argument fully. Suffice it to point out that its argument is closely similar to that which is found, for instance, in the Summa Contra Gentiles of Thomas Aquinas. Butler holds to an Arminian view in theology. He therefore assumes that the natural man by "a reasonable use of reason" can interpret aright "the course and constitution of nature." If only the natural man will continue to employ the same "reasonable use of reason" with respect to the facts presented to him in Scripture about Christ and his work there is every likelihood that he will become a Christian.

Less Consistent Calvinism

The question of starting point then is largely determined by one's theology. In the first chapters it has been our aim to set forth the salient features of Christianity according to the principles of the Reformed faith. In particular it has been the aim to indicate the main features of Christianity after the fashion indicated by the great Reformed theologians of recent times. It is on the basis of the work of such men as Charles Hodge and B.B.Warfield, to mention no others, that we have formulated the broad outline of the Reformed life and world view. It is only by the help of such men that we have been enabled to attain to anything like a consistent Protestantism.

It is only to follow out their suggestion then if we follow their principles in apologetics as well as in theology proper. We are to defend, as Warfield himself so well expresses it, not some minimal essence of Christianity, nor every detail included in the doctrines of Christianity, but "just Christianity itself, including all its 'details' and involving its 'essence' — in its unexplicated and uncompressed entirety..." (Studies in Theology, p. 9).

And this Christianity we must bring to those who are dead in trespasses and sins. "It is," says Warfield, "upon a field of the dead that the Sun of righteousness has risen, and the shouts that announce His advent fall on deaf ears: yea, even though the morning stars should again sing for joy and the air be palpitant with the echo of the great proclamation, their voice could not penetrate the ears of the dead. As we sweep our eyes over the world lying in its wickedness it is the valley of the prophet's vision which we see before us: a valley that is filled with bones, and lo! they are very dry. What benefit is there in proclaiming to dry bones even the greatest of redemptions? How shall we stand and cry, 'O, ye dry bones, hear ye the word of the Lord!' In vain the redemption, in vain its proclamation, unless there come a breath from heaven to breathe upon these slain that they may live" (op. cit., p. 43). "The Christian lives by virtue of the life that has been given to him, and prior to the inception of that life, of course, he has no power of action; and it is of the utmost importance that as Christian men we should not lower our testimony to this supernaturalness of our salvation" (op. cit., p. 45). Regeneration, we have seen Hodge argue, is unto knowledge, righteousness and holiness.

It would seem that we have dropped from this high plane to the level of evangelicalism when Hodge speaks of the office of reason in matters of religion. Under this heading he takes up three points. First he shows that reason is necessary as a tool for the reception of revelation. About this point there can be little cause for dispute. "Revelations cannot be made to brutes or to idiots" (Systematic Theology, Vol. I, p. 49). Second, Hodge argues that "Reason must judge of the credibility of a revelation" (p. 50). And "the credible is that which can be believed. Nothing is incredible but the impossible. What may be, may be rationally (i.e., on adequate grounds) believed." What then is impossible? Hodge replies: "(1) That is impossible which involves a contradiction; as, that a thing is and is not; that right is wrong, and wrong right. (2) It is impossible that God should do, approve, or command what is morally wrong. (3) It is impossible that He should require of us to believe what contradicts any of the laws of belief which He has impressed upon our nature. (4) It is impossible that one truth should contradict another. It is impossible, therefore, that God should reveal anything as true which contradicts any well authenticated truth, whether of intuition, experience, or previous revelation" (op. cit., p. 51). Third, Hodge continues, "Reason must judge of the evidences of a revelation." As "faith involves assent, and assent is conviction produced by evidence, it follows that faith without evidence is either irrational or impossible" (p. 53). The second and third prerogatives of reason, says Hodge, are approved by Scripture itself. Paul "recognized the paramount authority of the intuitive judgments of the mind" (p. 52), and "Jesus appealed to his works as evidence of the truth of his claims" (p. 53).

It is not our purpose here to deal fully with the question of reason and revelation. Suffice it to note the ambiguity that underlies this approach to the question of the point of contact. When Hodge speaks of <u>reason</u> he means "those laws of belief which God has implanted in our nature" (p. 52). Now it is true, of course, that God has planted such laws of belief into our very being. It is this point on which Calvin lays such great stress when he says that all men have a sense of deity. But the unbeliever does not accept the doctrine of his creation in the image of God. It is therefore impossible to appeal to the intellectual and moral nature of men, as <u>men themselves interpret this nature</u>, and say that it must judge of the credibility and evidence of revelation. For if this is done, we are virtually telling the natural man to accept just so much and no more of Christianity as, with his perverted concept of human nature, he cares to accept.

To use once again the illustration of the saw: the saw is in itself but a tool. Whether it will move at all and whether it will cut in the right direction depends upon the man operating it. So also reason, or intellect, is always the instrument of a person. And the person employing it is always either a believer or an unbeliever. If he is a believer, his reason has already been changed in its set, as Hodge has told us, by regeneration. It cannot then be the judge; it is now a part of the regenerated person, gladly subject to the authority of God. It has by God's grace permitted itself to be interpreted by God's revelation. If, on the other hand, the person using his reason is an unbeliever, then this person, using his reason, will certainly assume the position of judge with respect to the credibility and evidence of revelation, but he will also certainly find the Christian religion incredible because impossible and the evidence for it always inadequate. Hodge's own teaching on the blindness and hardness of the natural man corroborates this fact. To attribute to the natural man the right to judge by means of his reason of what is possible or impossible, or to judge by means of his moral nature of what is good or evil, is virtually to deny the "particularism" which, as Hodge no less than Warfield, believes to be the very hall-mark of a truly biblical theology. In such a case Christianity would not claim to interpret the reasoner himself. That reasoner would be taken as already having within himself, previous to his acceptance of Christianity, the ability rightly to interpret and rightly to employ the powers of his own nature. And this is the exact equivalent of the Arminian position when it claims that God made salvation objectively possible but did not actually save individual men.

The main difficulty with the position of Hodge on this matter of the point of contact, then, is that it does not clearly distinguish between the original and the fallen nature of man. Basically, of course, it is Hodge's intention to appeal to the original nature of man as it came forth from the hands of its creator. But he frequently argues as though that original nature can still be found as active in the "common consciousness" of men. Now there is a large element of truth in the contention that the common sense of man has not strayed so far from the truth as have the sophistications of the philosophers. Outspoken, blasphemous atheism is not usually found among the masses of men. But this does not take away the fact that all men are sinful in all the manifestations of their personality.

A comparison may tend to clarify this point. In the seventh chapter of Romans, Paul speaks of himself, though a believer, as having a law of sin within his members which often controls him against his will. His "new man" is the real man, the man in Christ Jesus. But his "old man" is the remnant of his sinful nature that has not been fully destroyed. Applying this analogy to the natural man we have the following. The sinner is the one whose "new man" is the man in alliance with Satan. But his "old man" is that which wars within his members against his will; it is his nature as he came forth from the hands of his creator. When the prodigal has left his father's house he is on the way to the swine-trough. But while on his way he has his misgivings. He seeks to make himself believe that his true nature consists in his self-assertion away from the father's house. But he kicks against the pricks. He sins against better knowledge.

Now it is quite in accord with the genius of Hodge's theology to appeal to the "old man" in the sinner and altogether out of accord with his theology to appeal to the "new man" in the sinner as though he would form a basically proper judgment on any question. Yet Hodge has failed to distinguish clearly between these two. Accordingly he does not clearly distinguish the Reformed from the evangelical and Roman Catholic views of the point of contact. Accordingly he also speaks about "reason" as something that seems to operate rightly wherever it is found. But the "reason" of sinful men will invariably act wrongly. Particularly is this true when they are confronted with the specific contents of Scripture. The natural man will invariably employ the tool

49

of his reason to reduce these contents to a naturalistic level. He must do so even in the interest of the principle of contradiction. For his own ultimacy is the most basic presupposition of his entire philosophy. It is upon this presupposition as its fulcrum that he uses the law of contradiction. If he is asked to use his reason as the judge of the credibility of the Christian revelation without at the same time being asked to renounce his view of himself as ultimate, then he is virtually asked to believe and to disbelieve in his own ultimacy at the same time and in the same sense. Moreover this same man, in addition to rejecting Chrsitianity in the name of the law of contradiction, will also reject it in the name of what he calls his intuition of freedom. By this he means virtually the same thing as his ultimacy. Speaking of the "philosophers" Calvin says, "The principle they set out with was that man could not be a rational animal unless he had a free choice of good and evil ... They also imagined that that distinction between virtue and vice was destroyed, if man did not of his own counsel arrange his life" (Institutes, I, 15:7). If such an one is asked to accept the position of Christianity, according to which his destiny is ultimately determined by the counsel of God, he is asked to accept what to him makes right wrong and wrong right.

It is only to follow out the lead which Hodge in his theology, following Calvin, has given, if we seek our point of contact not in any abstraction whatsoever, whether it be reason or intuition. No such abstraction exists in the universe of men. We always deal with concrete individual men. These men are sinners. They have "an axe to grind." They want to suppress the truth in unrighteousness. They will employ their reason for that purpose. And they are not formally illogical if, granted the assumption of man's ultimacy, they reject the teachings of Christianity. On the contrary, to be logically consistent they are bound to do so. This point will engage us more fully in the sequel. For the moment it must suffice to have shown how the apologist is not only untrue to his own doctrine of man as the creature of God, but also defeats his own purpose if he appeals to some form of the "common consciousness of man."

Before going on to discuss what appears to us to be a more truly biblical view of the problem of the point of contact, we would call attention to one other form of inconsistent Calvinism on this matter. In his book Het Testimonium Spiritus Sancti, D. Valentine Hepp speaks about prima principia with respect to God, man, and the world which, he says, men in general accept. "With respect to the central truths which speak to us from creation as such, there is little doubt among men. A few mistaken scientists, who insist on maintaining their mistaken starting point, insist that they doubt whether God or man or world exist. They owe such statements, not to experience, but to their systems. But their number, though we hear much of them, is very small. Taken as a whole mankind does not deny the central truths. The great majority of men recognize a higher power above them, and do not hesitate to accept the reality of the world and of man" (p. 165). The position of Hepp, as appears even from this one quotation, is similar to that of

Hodge. Like Hodge, Hepp wants to appeal to a general faith in "central truths" that all men, when not too sophisticated, accept. There seems to be for Hepp, as for Hodge, something in the way of a common sense philosophy which the natural man has and which, because intuitive or spontaneous is, so far forth, not tainted by sin. It appears, however, even from the brief quotation given, that the "common notions" of men are sinful notions. For man to reflect on his own awareness of meaning and then merely to say that a higher power, a God, exists, is in effect to say that God does not exist. It is as though a child, reflecting upon his home environment would conclude that a father or a mother exist. And to "recognize the reality of the world and of man" is in itself not even to recognize the elemental truths of creation and providence. It is not enough to appeal from the more highly articulated systems of non-Christian thinkers to the philosophy of the common consciousness, of common sense, of intuition, to something that is more immediately related to the revelational pressure that rests upon men. Both Hepp and Hodge seem to be desirous of doing no more than Calvin does when he appeals to the sense of deity present in all men. But this notion, seeking to set forth as it does the teaching of Paul, that God's revelation is present to every man, must be carefully distinguished from the reaction that sinful men make to this revelation. The revelation of God, not of a God, is so immediately present to every man, that as Warfield, following Calvin, says: "The conviction of the existence of God bears the marks of an intuitive truth in so far as it is the universal and unavoidable belief of men, and is given in the very same act with the idea of self, which is known at once as dependent and responsible and this implies one on whom it depends and to whom it is responsible" (Studies in Theology, p. 110). It is to this sense of deity, even this knowledge of God, which, Paul tells us (Romans 1:19-20) every man has, but which, as Paul also tells us, every sinner seeks to suppress, that the Christian apologetic must appeal.

The Dilemma of the Roman Catholic View

What has been said up to this point may seem to be discouraging in the extreme. It would seem that the argument up to this point has driven us to a denial of any point of contact whatsoever with the unbeliever. Is it not true that men must have some contact with the truth if they are to receive further knowledge of it? If men are totally ignorant of the truth how can they even become interested in it? If men are totally blind why display before them the colors of the spectrum? If they are deaf why take them to the academy of music?

Moreover, is not reason itself a gift of God? And does not the scientist, though not a Christian, know much about the universe? Does one need to be a Christian to know that two times two are four? And besides all this, does Christianity, while telling us of much that is above reason, require of us to accept anything that is against reason?

51

Our answer to this type of query is that it is precisely in the Reformed conception of the point of contact, and in it alone, that the historically so famous dilemma about the wholly ignorant, or the wholly omniscient, can be avoided. But before showing this positively it is necessary to indicate that in the Roman Catholic view this dilemma is insoluble.

If a man is wholly ignorant of the truth he cannot be interested in the truth. On the other hand if he is really interested in the truth it must be that he already possesses the main elements of the truth. It is in the interest of escaping the horns of this dilemma that Rome and evangelical Protestantism seek a point of contact in some area of "common knowledge" between believers and unbelievers. Their argument is that in teaching the total depravity of man in the way he does the Calvinist is in the unfortunate position of having to speak to deaf men when he preaches the gospel. We believe, on the contrary, that it is only the Calvinist who is not in this position.

Plato's famous allegory of the cave may illustrate the Roman Catholic position. The dwellers of this cave had chains about their necks and on their legs. They saw nothing but shadows and attributed echoes to these shadows. Yet they supposed that "they were naming what was actually before them." If one of them should be released, says Plato, he would need to get accustomed to the light of the sun. But he would pity those who were still in the cave. And "if he had to compete in measuring the shadows with the prisoners who have never moved out of the den ... would he not be ridiculous" in their view? "Men would say of him that up he went and down he comes without his eyes; and that there is no use in even thinking of ascending; and if anyone tried to loose another and lead him up to the light, let them only catch the offender in the act, and they would put him to death."

Plato himself interprets this allegory in relation to man's capacity for and knowledge of the truth. The prisoners have eyes with which to see the truth; all they need is to have their heads turned about so they may face the truth.

It is in some such fashion that Rome thinks of the natural man. Following Aristotle's general method of reasoning, Thomas Aquinas argues that the natural man can, by the ordinary use of his reason, do justice to the natural revelation that surrounds him. He merely needs some assistance in order that he may also see and react properly to the supernatural revelation that is found in Christianity.

According to the Roman view then, the natural man is already in possession of the truth. To be sure, he is said to be in possession of the truth only with respect to natural revelation. But if the natural man can and does interpret natural revelation in a way that is essentially correct there is no reason why he should need supernatural aid in order to interpret Christianity truly. At most he would need the information that Christ and his Spirit have come into the world. Hearing this news he would not fail, as a rational being, to make the proper reaction to it. If the natural man's eyes (reason) enable him to see correctly in one dimension, there is no good reason to think that these same eyes will not enable him, without further assistance from without, to see correctly in all dimensions. There would be no reason why all of the prisoners of the cave could not break their chains and walk in the light of day. In fact, Plato gives no reason why those who did not escape could not have escaped as well as the one who did.

On the other hand, it may be said that according to the Roman Catholic view the natural man does not give a fully correct interpretation of natural revelation. Does not Thomas Aquinas correct the interpretations that "the philosopher" has given of the things of nature? And does not the Roman Catholic view of the image of God in man itself imply that even originally, before the fall, man was unable, without the bonum superadditum to know anything in a perfect way?

We reply that though Aquinas does correct some of the conclusions of Aristotle, he accepts the method of Aristotle as essentially sound. But, ignoring this, and granting for the sake of the argument that according to Rome the natural man's view of natural revelation is not fully correct, it should be noted that the only reason Rome can adduce for this fact is a defect in revelation itself. The prisoners of Plato's cave are not to be blamed for the fact that they see shadows only. They are doing full justice by the position in which they find themselves. If their heads are bound so that they see shadows only, this is due to no fault of theirs. It is due to the constitution and course of nature. According to this view the human mind is not originally and naturally in contact with the truth. The idea of freedom, as entertained by Roman theology, is based upon man's being metaphysically distinct from "god." And this is tantamount to saying that man is free to the extent that he has no "being." There is on this basis no genuine point of contact with the mind of the natural man at all.

We do not object to the idea that the mind of man is said to be always in need of supernatural revelation. On the contrary we would stress the fact that even in paradise the mind of man needed and enjoyed a supernatural revelation. What we object to is the reason given for the need that man had of supernatural revelation even in paradise. The reason for this need, according to the Roman Catholic view, is virtually a defect in the original constitution of man. This implies that man is naturally, according to his original constitution, prone to error as well as to truth. The reason for this is that the god of Roman Catholicism does not control "whatsoever comes to pass." Man is, accordingly, not exclusively confronted with that which reveals God. Man is also confronted with the ultimately non-rational. On such a conception of reality in general it is natural that man's constitution should be thought of, on the one hand, as of itself possessing the truth, and, on the

53

other hand, as never able, by its natural action, to come into possession of the truth.

On such a basis too, the addition of supernatural to natural revelation would not remedy matters. It would be as true of supernatural as of natural revelation that either it would not reach man or else if it did reach man he would not be in need of it.

If natural revelation does not so envelop man as to make it impossible for him to look at anything that does not speak of God, then supernatural revelation will not do this either. If natural revelation does not speak of such a God as by his counsel surrounds man completely, then neither can supernatural revelation speak of such a God. But if it did, per impossible, speak of such a God, it could mean nothing to the mind of man as Rome conceives of it. The revelation of a self-sufficient God can have no meaning for a mind that thinks of itself as ultimately autonomous. The possibility for a point of contact has disappeared. The whole idea of the revelation of the self-sufficient God of Scripture drops to the ground if man himself is autonomous or self-sufficient. If man is not himself revelational in the internal structure of his being, he can receive no revelation that comes to him from without.

On the other hand, if man is in any sense autonomous he is not in need of revelation. If he is then said to possess the truth he possesses it as the product of the ultimately legislative powers of his intellect. It is only if he can virtually control by means of the application of the law of non-contradiction all the facts of reality that surround him, that he can know any truth at all. And thus, if he knows any truth in this way, he, in effect, knows all truth.

On the Roman Catholic position, then, man is, with the cave-dwellers of Plato, by virtue of his own constitution, adapted to semi-darkness. Revelation would not do him any good, even though we might think of him as in need of it. If revelation is to come to him, it must come to him as the truth came to one of Plato's cave-dwellers, in an accidental fashion. Or else man is, with the accidentally liberated cave-dweller of Plato, not in need of supernatural revelation; potentially he has all truth within his reach.

The Reformed Position

The fully biblical conception of the point of contact, it ought now to be clear, is the only one that can escape the dilemma of absolute ignorance or absolute omniscience.

The one great defect of the Roman Catholic view and the Arminian view is, as noted, that it ascribes ultimacy or self-sufficiency to the mind of man. Romanism and Arminianism do this in their views of man as stated

54

in their works on systematic theology. It is consistent for them, therefore, not to challenge the assumption of ultimacy as this is made by the non-believer. But Reformed theology, as worked out by Calvin and his recent exponents such as Hodge, Warfield, Kuyper and Bavinck, holds that man's mind is derivative. As such it is naturally in contact with God's revelation. It is surrounded by nothing but revelation. It is itself inherently revelational. It cannot naturally be conscious of itself without being conscious of its creatureliness. For man self-consciousness presupposes God-consciousness. Calvin speaks of this as man's inescapable sense of deity.

For Adam in paradise God-consciousness could not come in at the end of a syllogistic process of reasoning. God-consciousness was for him the presupposition of the significance of his reasoning on anything.

To the doctrine of creation must be added the conception of the covenant. Man was created as a historical being. God placed upon him from the outset of history the responsibility and task of reinterpreting the counsel of God as expressed in creation to himself individually and collectively. Man's creature-consciousness may therefore be more particularly signalized as covenant-consciousness. But the revelation of the covenant to man in paradise was supernaturally mediated. This was naturally the case inasmuch as it pertained to man's historical task. Thus, the sense of obedience or disobedience was immediately involved in Adam's consciousness of himself. Covenant consciousness envelops creature-consciousness. In paradise Adam knew that as a creature of God it was natural and proper that he should keep the covenant that God had made with him. In this way it appears that man's proper self-consciousness depended, even in paradise upon his being in contact with both supernatural and natural revelation. God's natural revelation was within man as well as about him. Man's very constitution as a rational and moral being is itself revelational to man as the ethically responsible reactor to revelation. And natural revelation is itself incomplete. It needed from the outset to be supplemented with supernatural revelation about man's future. Thus the very idea of supernatural revelation is correlatively embodied in the idea of man's proper self-consciousness.

It is in this way that man may be said to be by his original constitution in contact with the truth while yet not in possession of all the truth. Man is not in Plato's cave. He is not in the anomalous position of having eyes with which to see while yet he dwells in darkness. He has not, as was the case with the cave-dwellers of Plato, some mere capacity for the truth that might never come to fruition. Man had originally not merely a capacity for receiving the truth; he was in actual possession of the truth. The world of truth was not found in some realm far distant from him; it was right before him. That which spoke to his senses no less than that which spoke to his intellect was the voice of God. Even when he closed his eyes upon the external world his internal sense would manifest God to him in his own constitution. The matter of his experience was in no sense a mere form with which he might organize the raw material. On the contrary, the <u>matter</u> of his experience was lit up through and through. Yet it was lit up for him by the voluntary activity of God whose counsel made things to be what they are. Man could not be aware of himself without also being aware of objects about him and without also being aware of his responsibility to manage himself and all things for the glory of God. Man's consciousness of objects and of self was not static. It was consciousness in <u>time</u>. Moreover, consciousness of objects and of self in time meant consciousness of <u>history</u> in relationship to the plan of God back of history. Man's first sense of self-awareness implied the awareness of the presence of God as the one for whom he has a great task to accomplish.

It is only when we begin our approach to the question of the point of contact by thus analyzing the situation as it obtained in paradise before the fall of man that we can attain to a true conception of the natural man and his capacities with respect to the truth. The apostle Paul speaks of the natural man as actually possessing the knowledge of God (Rom. 1:19-21). The greatness of his sin lies precisely in the fact that ''when they knew God, they glorified him not as God.'' No man can escape knowing God. It is indelibly involved in his awareness of anything whatsoever. Man <u>ought</u>, therefore, as Calvin puts it, to recognize God. There is no excuse for him if he does not. The reason for his failure to recognize God lies exclusively in him. It is due to his wilfull transgression of the very law of his being.

Neither Romanism nor Protestant evangelicalism can do full justice to this teaching of Paul. In effect both of them fail to surround man exclusively with God's revelation. Not holding to the counsel of God as all-controlling they cannot teach that man's self-awareness always pre-supposes awareness of God. According to both Rome and evangelicalism man may have some measure of awareness of objects about him and of himself in relation to them without being aware at the same time of his responsibility to manipulate both of them in relation to God. Thus man's consciousness of objects, of self, of time and of history are not from the outset brought into an exclusive relationship of dependence upon God. <u>Hinc</u> <u>illae</u> <u>lacrimae</u>!

Of course, when we thus stress Paul's teaching that all men do not merely have a capacity for but are in actual possession of the knowledge of God, we have at once to add Paul's further instruction to the effect that all men, due to the sin within them, always and in all relationships seek to ''suppress'' this knowledge of God (Rom. 1:18 <u>American</u> <u>Standard</u> <u>Version</u>). The natural man is such an one as constantly throws water on a fire he cannot quench. He has yielded to the temptation of Satan, and has become his bondservant. When Satan tempted Adam and Eve in paradise he sought to make them believe that man's self-consciousness was ultimate rather than derivative and God-dependent. He argued, as it were, that it was of the nature of self-consciousness to make itself the final reference point of all predication. He argued, as it were, that God had no control over all that

might come forth in the process of time. That is to say, he argued, in effect, that as any form of self-consciousness must assume its own ultimacy,
so it must also admit its own limitation in the fact that much that happens
is under no control at all. Thus Satan argued, as it were, that man's consciousness of time and of time's products in history is, if intelligible at all,
intelligible in some measure independently of God.

Romanism and evangelicalism, however, do not attribute this assumption of autonomy or ultimacy on the part of man as due to sin. They hold that
man should quite properly think of himself and of his relation to objects in
time in this way. Hence they do injustice to Paul's teaching with respect to
the effect of sin on the interpretative activity of man. As they virtually deny
that originally man not merely had a capacity for the truth but was in actual
possession of the truth, so also they virtually deny that the natural man suppresses the truth.

It is not to be wondered at then that neither Rome nor evangelicalism
are little interested in challenging the "philosophers" when these, as Calvin
says, interpret man's consciousness without being aware of the tremendous
difference in man's attitude toward the truth before and after the fall. Accordingly they do not distinguish carefully between the natural man's own
conception of himself and the biblical conception of him. Yet for the question of the point of contact this is all-important. If we make our appeal to
the natural man without being aware of this distinction we virtually admit
that the natural man's estimate of himself is correct. We may, to be sure,
even then, maintain that he is in need of information. We may even admit
that he is morally corrupt. But the one thing which, on this basis, we cannot admit, is that his claim to be able to interpret at least some area of
experience in a way that is essentially correct, is mistaken. We cannot
then challenge his most basic epistemological assumption to the effect that
his self-consciousness and time-consciousness are self-explanatory. We
cannot challenge his right to interpret all his experience in exclusively
immanentistic categories. And on this everything hinges. For if we first
allow the legitimacy of the natural man's assumption of himself as the ultimate reference point in interpretation in any dimension we cannot deny
his right to interpret Christianity itself in naturalistic terms.

The point of contact for the gospel, then, must be sought within the
natural man. Deep down in his mind every man knows that he is the creature of God and responsible to God. Every man, at bottom, knows that he
is a covenant-breaker. But every man acts and talks as though this were
not so. It is the one point that cannot bear mentioning in his presence. A
man may have internal cancer. Yet it may be the one point he will not have
one speak of in his presence. He will grant that he is not feeling well. He
will accept any sort of medication so long as it does not pretend to be given
in answer to a cancer diagnosis. Will a good doctor cater to him on this
matter? Certainly not. He will tell his patient that he has promise of life,

but promise of life on one condition, that is, of an immediate internal operation. So it is with the sinner. He is alive but alive as a covenant-breaker. But his own interpretative activity with respect to all things proceeds on the assumption that such is not the case. Romanism and evangelicalism, by failing to appeal exclusively to that which is within man but is also suppressed by every man, virtually allow the legitimacy of the natural man's view of himself. They do not seek to explode the last stronghold to which the natural man always flees and where he always makes his final stand. They cut off the weeds at the surface but do not dig up the roots of these weeds, for fear that crops will not grow.

The truly biblical view, on the other hand, applies atomic power and flame-throwers to the very presupposition of the natural man's ideas with respect to himself. It does not fear to lose a point of contact by uprooting the weeds rather than by cutting them off at the very surface. It is assured of a point of contact in the fact that every man is made in the image of God and has impressed upon him the law of God. In that fact alone he may rest secure with respect to the point of contact problem. For that fact makes men always accessible to God. That fact assures us that every man, to be a man at all, must already be in contact with the truth. He is so much in contact with the truth that much of his energy is spent in the vain effort to hide this fact from himself. His efforts to hide this fact from himself are bound to be self-frustrative.

Only by thus finding the point of contact in man's sense of deity that lies underneath his own conception of self-consciousness as ultimate can we be both true to Scripture and effective in reasoning with the natural man.

CHAPTER IV

THE PROBLEM OF METHOD

A discussion of the problem of methodology naturally follows upon that of the problem of the point of contact. If we have discovered what we shall think of the person to whom we are to make our address in the interest of winning him to an acceptance of Christianity, we must next inquire as to the way by which we shall lead him to a knowledge of the truth.

But we were unable to agree with the natural man in his estimate of himself. It is not likely then that we shall be able to agree with him on the problem of method. For it is true no less of method than it is of the starting point that it is involved in the position to be defended. The Christian view of man and the Christian view of method are alike aspects of the Christian position as a whole. So also the non-Christian view of man and the non-Christian view of method are alike aspects of the non-Christian position as a whole. That such is indeed the case will appear as we proceed. For the moment the point is dogmatically asserted in order to indicate the plan of procedure for this chapter.

Our concern throughout is to indicate the nature of a truly Protestant, that is, a Reformed apologetic. A Reformed method of apologetics must seek to vindicate the Reformed life and world view as Christianity come to its own. It has already become plain that this implies a refusal to grant that any area or aspect of reality, any fact or any law of nature or of history, can be correctly interpreted except it be seen in the light of the main doctrines of Christianity. But if this be true, it becomes quite impossible for the apologist to do what Roman Catholics and Arminians can and must do on the basis of their view of Christianity, namely, agree with the non-Christian in his principles of methodology to see whether or not Christian theism be true. From the Roman Catholic and the Arminian point of view the question of methodology, like that of starting point, is a neutral matter. According to these positions the Christian apologist can legitimately join the non-Christian scientist or philosopher as he, by his recognized methods, investigates certain dimensions of reality. Neither the follower of Thomas Aquinas nor the follower of the "judicious Butler" would <u>need</u>, on his principles, to object when, for instance, A.E.Taylor says: "Natural science, let me say again, is exclusively concerned with the detection of 'laws of nature,' uniformities of sequence in the course of events. The typical form of such a law is the statement that whenever certain definitely measurable events occur some other measurable event will also be found to occur. Any enquiry thus delimited obviously can throw no light on the question whether God exists or not, the question whether the whole course of events among which the man of science discovers these uniformities of sequence is or is not guided by a supreme intelligence to the production of an intrinsically good result'' (Does God Exist? pp. 13, 14, London, 1947). The Reformed apologist, on the other hand, would compromise what he holds to be of the essence of Christianity if he agreed with Taylor. For him the whole of created reality, including therefore the fields of research with which the various sciences deal, reveals the same God of which Scripture speaks. The very essence of created reality is its revelational character. Scientists deal with that which has the imprint of God's face upon it. Created reality may be compared to a great estate. The owner has his name plainly and indelibly written at unavoidable places. How then would it be possible for some stranger to enter this estate, make researches in it, and then fairly say that in these researches he need not and cannot be confronted with the question of ownership? To change the figure, compare the facts of nature and history, the facts with which the sciences are concerned, to a linoleum that has its figure indelibly imprinted in it. The pattern of such a linoleum cannot be effaced till the linoleum itself is worn away. Thus inescapably does the scientist meet the pattern of Christian theism in each fact with which he deals. The apostle Paul lays great stress upon the fact that man is without excuse if he does not discover God in nature. Following Paul's example Calvin argues that men ought to see God, not a God, not some supernatural power, but the only God, in nature. They have not done justice by the facts they see displayed before and within them if they say that a God exists or that God probably exists. The Calvinist holds to the essential perspicuity of natural as well as biblical revelation. This does not imply that a non-Christian and a non-theistic interpretation of reality cannot be made to appear plausible. But it does mean that no non-Christian position can be made to appear more than merely plausible.

Roman Catholic apologists can, therefore, to the extent that their own theology does not teach the perspicuity of natural revelation, with consistency use the method of the natural man. Just as Rome, having a semi-pagan conception of the nature of man, can agree with the natural man's conception of the starting point in knowledge, so also, having a semi-pagan concept of the nature of the objects man must know, he can, to a large extent, agree with the natural man's conception of the method of knowledge.

Arminian apologists also, to the extent that their theology is faulty, can consistently agree with the non-believer on the question of methodology. Believing to some extent in the autonomy and ultimacy of human personality Arminianism can, in a measure, agree on the question of starting-point with those who make men the final reference point in all human predication. So also, believing to some extent in the existence of facts that are not wholly under the control and direction of the counsel of God, Arminianism can agree on the question of method with those for whom the object of knowledge has nothing at all to do with the plan of God.

In contradistinction from both Roman Catholics and Arminians, however, the Reformed apologist cannot agree at all with the methodology of the natural man. Disagreeing with the natural man's interpretation of himself as the ultimate reference point, the Reformed apologist must seek his point of contact with the natural man in that which is beneath the threshold of his working consciousness, in the sense of deity which he seeks to suppress. And to do this the Reformed apologist must also seek a point of contact with the systems constructed by the natural man. But this point of contact must be in the nature of a head-on collision. If there is no head-on collision with the systems of the natural man there will be no point of contact with the sense of deity in the natural man. So also, disagreeing with the natural man on the nature of the object of knowledge, the Reformed apologist must disagree with him on the method to be employed in acquiring knowledge. According to the doctrine of the Reformed faith all the facts of nature and of history are what they are, do what they do, and undergo what they undergo, in accord with the one comprehensive counsel of God. All that may be known by man is already known by God. And it is already known by God because it is controlled by God.

The significance of this for the question of method will be pointed out soon. For the moment this simple fact must be signalized as the reason which precludes the possibility of agreement on methodology between the Reformed theologian and the non-Christian philosopher or scientist. We may mention one point that brings out the difference in methodology between the two positions. It is the point with reference to the relevancy of hypotheses. For the non-Christian any sort of hypothesis may, at the outset of an investigation, be as relevant as any other. This is so because on a non-Christian basis facts are not already what they are because of the systematic relation they sustain to God. On a non-Christian basis facts are "rationalized" for the first time when interpreted by man. But for one who holds that the facts are already part of an ultimately rational system by virtue of the plan of God it is clear that such hypotheses as presuppose the non-existence of such a plan must, even from the outset of his investigation, be considered irrelevant.

Reasoning by Presupposition

These things being as they are it will be our first task in this chapter to show that a consistently Christian method of apologetic argument, in agreement with its own basic conception of the starting point, must be by presupposition. To argue by presupposition is to indicate what are the epistemological and metaphysical principles that underlie and control one's method. The Reformed apologist will frankly admit that his own methodology presupposes the truth of Christian theism. Basic to all the doctrines of Christian theism is that of the self-contained God, or, if we wish, that of the ontological Trinity. It is this notion of the ontological Trinity that ultimately controls a truly Christian methodology. Based upon this notion of the ontological Trinity and consistent with it, is the concept of the counsel of God according to which all things in the created world are regulated.

Christian methodology is therefore based upon presuppositions that are quite the opposite of those of the non-Christian. It is claimed to be of the very essence of any non-Christian form of methodology that it cannot be determined in advance to what conclusions it must lead. To assert, as the Christian apologist is bound to do if he is not to deny the very thing he is seeking to establish, that the conclusion of a true method is the truth of Christian theism is, from the point of view of the non-Christian, the clearest evidence of authoritarianism. In spite of this claim to neutrality on the part of the non-Christian the Reformed apologist must point out that every method, the supposedly neutral one no less than any other, presupposes either the truth or the falsity of Christian theism.

The method of reasoning by presupposition may be said to be indirect rather than direct. The issue between believers and non-believers in Christian theism cannot be settled by a direct appeal to "facts" or "laws" whose nature and significance is already agreed upon by both parties to the debate. The question is rather as to what is the final reference-point required to make the "facts" and "laws" intelligible. The question is as to what the "facts" and "laws" really are. Are they what the non-Christian methodology assumes that they are? Are they what the Christian theistic methodology presupposes they are?

The answer to this question cannot be finally settled by any direct discussion of "facts." It must, in the last analysis be settled indirectly. The Christian apologist must place himself upon the position of his opponent, assuming the correctness of his method merely for argument's sake, in order to show him that on such a position the "facts" are not facts and the "laws" are not laws. He must also ask the non-Christian to place himself upon the Christian position for argument's sake in order that he may be shown that only upon such a basis do "facts" and "laws" appear intelligible.

To admit one's own presuppositions and to point out the presuppositions of others is therefore to maintain that all reasoning is, in the nature of the case, circular reasoning. The starting point , the method, and the conclusion are always involved in one another.

Let us say that the Christian apologist has placed the position of Christian theism before his opponent. Let us say further that he has pointed out that his own method of investigation of reality presupposes the truth of his position. This will appear to his friend whom he is seeking to win to an acceptance of the Christian position as highly authoritarian and out of accord with the proper use of human reason. What will the apologist do next? If he is a Roman Catholic or an Arminian he will tone down the nature of Christianity to some extent in order to make it appear that the consistent application of his friend's neutral method will lead to an acceptance of Christian theism after all. But if he is a Calvinist this way is not open to him. He will point out that the more consistently his friend applies his supposedly neutral method the more certainly he will come to the conclusion that Christian theism is not true. Roman Catholics and Arminians, appealing to the "reason" of the natural man as the natural man himself interprets his reason, namely as autonomous, are bound to use the direct method of approach to the natural man, the method that assumes the essential correctness of a non-Christian and non-theistic conception of reality. The Reformed apologist, on the other hand, appealing to that knowledge of the true God in the natural man which the natural man suppresses by means of his assumption of ultimacy, will also appeal to the knowledge of the true method which the natural man knows but suppresses. The natural man at bottom knows that he is the creature of God. He knows also that he is responsible to God. He knows that he should live to the glory of God. He knows that in all that he does he should stress that the field of reality which he investigates has the stamp of God's ownership upon it. But he suppresses his knowledge of himself as he truly is. He is the man with the iron mask. A true method of apologetics must seek to tear off that iron mask. The Roman Catholic and the Arminian make no attempt to do so. They even flatter its wearer about his fine appearance. In the introductions of their books on apologetics Arminian as well as Roman Catholic apologists frequently seek to set their "opponents" at ease by assuring them that their method, in its field, is all that any Christian could desire. In contradistinction from this, the Reformed apologist will point out again and again that the only method that will lead to the truth in any field is that method which recognizes the fact that man is a creature of God, that he must therefore seek to think God's thoughts after him.

It is not as though the Reformed apologist should not interest himself in the nature of the non-Christian's method. On the contrary he should make a critical analysis of it. He should, as it were, join his "friend" in the use of it. But he should do so self-consciously with the purpose of showing that its most consistent application not merely leads away from Christian theism but in leading away from Christian theism leads to destruction of reason and science as well.

An illustration may indicate more clearly what is meant. Suppose we think of a man made of water in an infinitely extended ocean of water. Desiring to get out of water, he makes a ladder of water. He sets this ladder upon the water and against the water and then climbs out of the water only to fall into the water. So hopeless and senseless a picture must be drawn of the natural man's methodology based as it is upon the assumption that time or chance is ultimate. On his assumption his own rationality is a product of chance. On his assumption even the laws of logic which he employs are products of chance. The rationality and purpose that he may be searching for are still bound to be products of chance. So then the Christian apologist, whose position requires him to hold that Christian theism is really true and as such must be taken as the presupposition which alone makes the acquisition of knowledge in any field intelligible, must join his "friend" in his hopeless gyrations so as to point out to him that his efforts are always in vain.

63

It will then appear that Christian theism, which was first rejected because of its supposed authoritarian character, is the only position which gives human reason a field for successful operation and a method of true progress in knowledge.

Two remarks may here be made by way of meeting the most obvious objections that will be raised to this method of the Reformed apologist. The first objection that suggests itself may be expressed in the rhetorical question "Do you mean to assert that non-Christians do not discover truth by the methods they employ?" The reply is that we mean nothing so absurd as that. The implication of the method here advocated is simply that non-Christians are never able and therefore never do employ their own methods consistently. Says A.E. Taylor in discussing the question of the uniformity of nature, "The fundamental thought of modern science, at any rate until yesterday, was that there is a 'universal reign of law' throughout nature. Nature is rational in the sense that it has everywhere a coherent pattern which we can progressively detect by the steady application of our own intelligence to the scrutiny of natural processes. Science has been built up all along on the basis of this principle of the 'uniformity of nature,' and the principle is one which science itself has no means of demonstrating. No one could possibly prove its truth to an opponent who seriously disputed it. For all attempts to produce the 'evidence' for the 'uniformity of nature' themselves presuppose the very principle they are intended to prove" (Does God Exist? p. 2). Our argument as over against this would be that the existence of the God of Christian theism and the conception of his counsel as controlling all things in the universe is the only presupposition which can account for the uniformity of nature which the scientist needs. But the best and only possible proof for the existence of such a God is that his existence is required for the uniformity of nature and for the coherence of all things in the world. We cannot prove the existence of beams underneath a floor if by proof we mean that they must be ascertainable in the way that we can see the chairs and tables of the room. But the very idea of a floor as the support of tables and chairs requires the idea of beams that are underneath. But there would be no floor if no beams were underneath. Thus there is absolutely certain proof for the existence of God and the truth of Christian theism. Even non-Christians presuppose its truth while they verbally reject it. They need to presuppose the truth of Christian theism in order to account for their own accomplishments.

The second objection may be voiced in the following words: "While a Christian can prove that his Christian position is fully as reasonable as the opponent's view, there is no such thing as an absolutely compelling proof that God exists, or that the Bible is the word of God, just as little as anyone can prove its opposite." In this way of putting the matter there is a confusion between what is objectively valid and what is subjectively acceptable to the natural man. It is true that no method of argument for Christianity will be acceptable to the natural man. Moreover, it is true that the

more consistently Christian our methodology, the less acceptable it will be
to the natural man. We find something similar in the field of theology. It
is precisely the Reformed faith which, among other things, teaches the total
depravity of the natural man, which is most loathsome to that natural man.
But this does not prove that the Reformed faith is not true. A patient may
like a doctor who tells him that his disease can be cured by means of external
applications and dislike the doctor who tells him that he needs a major internal operation. Yet the latter doctor may be right in his diagnosis. It is the
weakness of the Roman Catholic and the Arminian methods that they virtually
identify objective validity with subjective acceptability to the natural man.
Distinguishing carefully between these two, the Reformed apologist maintains
that there is an absolutely valid argument for the existence of God and for the
truth of Christian theism. He cannot do less without virtually admitting that
God's revelation to man is not clear. It is fatal for the Reformed apologist
to admit that man has done justice to the objective evidence if he comes to
any other conclusion than that of the truth of Christian theism.

As for the question whether the natural man will accept the truth of
such an argument, we answer that he will if God pleases by his Spirit to take
the scales from his eyes and the mask from his face. It is upon the power
of the Holy Spirit that the Reformed preacher relies when he tells men that
they are lost in sin and in need of a Savior. The Reformed preacher does
not tone down his message in order that it may find acceptance with the natural man. He does not say that his message is less certainly true because
of its non-acceptance by the natural man. The natural man is, by virtue
of his creation in the image of God, always accessible to the truth; accessible
to the penetration of the truth by the Spirit of God. Apologetics, like systematics, is valuable to the precise extent that it presses the truth upon the
attention of the natural man. The natural man must be blasted out of his
hideouts, his caves, his last lurking places. Neither Roman Catholic nor
Arminian methodologies have the flame-throwers with which to reach him.
In the all-out war between the Christian and the natural man as he appears
in modern garb it is only the atomic energy of a truly Reformed methodology
that will explode the last Festung to which the Roman Catholic and the Arminian always permit him to retreat and to dwell in safety.

Scripture

It has been pointed out that the difference between a Roman Catholic-
Arminian type of argument and a Reformed type of argument lies in the fact
that the former is direct and the latter is indirect. The former grants the
essential truthfulness of the non-Christian theory of man and of method,
while the latter challenges both. This difference will appear again and appear in its fundamental importance still more strikingly if the question of
the place of Scripture in apologetics is brought up for consideration. A few
remarks on this subject must suffice.

For better or for worse the Protestant apologist is committed to the doctrine of Scripture as the infallibly inspired final revelation of God to man. This being the case, he is committed to the defense of Christian theism as a unit. For him theism is not really theism unless it is Christian theism. The Protestant apologist cannot be concerned to prove the existence of any other God than the one who has spoken to man authoritatively and finally through Scripture.

The entire debate about theism will be purely formal unless theism be taken as the foundation of Christianity. But if it is so taken it is no longer theism as such but Christian theism that is in debate. Pantheists, deists, and theists, that is bare theists, may formally agree that God exists. Socrates, in arguing about the nature of piety with Euthyphro says that men "join issue about particular." So if the whole debate in apologetics is to be more than a meaningless discussion about the that of God's existence and is to go on to a consideration of what kind of God exists, then the question of God's revelation to man must be brought into the picture. Even before the entrance of sin, as already noted, man required supernatural positive revelation as a supplement to revelation in the created universe around and within him. To understand God's general revelation in the universe aright it was imperative for man that he see this revelation in relationship to a higher revelation with respect to the final destiny of man and the universe. If then even man in paradise could read nature aright only in connection with and in the light of supernatural positive revelation, how much the more is this true of man after the fall. In paradise the supernatural revelation of God to man told him that if he would eat of the forbidden tree he would surely die. Having eaten of this fruit he could therefore expect nothing but eternal separation from God as his final destiny. Of God's intention to save a people for his own precious possession he could learn nothing from nature. Nor was this involved in the pre-redemptive supernatural revelation that had been vouchsafed to him in paradise. It had to come by way of post-lapsarian supernatural revelation. Covenant-breakers could expect nothing but covenant wrath. That God meant to bring covenant-breakers back into covenant communion with himself through the covenant of grace could in no wise be discovered other than by supernatural redemptive revelation. B.B. Warfield brings out this point when he says that in addition to believing the supernatural fact, that is, God as a transcendent, self-existent being and in the supernatural act exemplified in creation and providence, the Christian must also believe in supernatural redemption. "As certainly as the recognition of the great fact of sin is an element in the Christian's world-conception, the need and therefore the actuality of the direct corrective act of God — of miracle, in a word — enters ineradicably into his belief" (Studies in Theology, p. 38).

But supernatural redemption in itself would not be of any avail. "For how should we be advantaged by a supernatural redemption of which we knew nothing? Who is competent to uncover to us the meaning of this great series of redemptive acts but God himself? ... Two thousand years ago a child was born in Bethlehem, who throve and grew up nobly, lived a life of poverty and beneficence, was cruelly slain and rose from the dead. What is that to us? After a little, as his followers sat waiting in Jerusalem, there was a rush as of a mighty wind, and an appearance of tongues of fire descending upon their heads. Strange: but what concern have we in it all? We require the revealing Word to tell us who and what this goodly child was, why he lived and what he wrought by his death, what it meant that he could not be holden of the grave, and what those cloven tongues of fire signified ... before they can avail as redemptive facts to us" (Warfield, idem, p. 42). Going a bit beyond this it may be asserted that sinful man would naturally want to destroy a supernatural revelation that portrays his sin and shame and tells him that he is helpless and undone. This is out of accord with the pride that is a prime mark of sin. Hence the necessity for the inscripturation of the God-given interpretation of post-lapsarian supernatural revelation of God to man.

Thus the Bible, as the infallibly inspired revelation of God to sinful man, stands before us as that light in terms of which all the facts of the created universe must be interpreted. All of finite existence, natural and redemptive, functions in relation to one all-inclusive plan that is in the mind of God. Whatever insight man is to have into this pattern of the activity of God he must attain by looking at all his objects of research in the light of Scripture. "If true religion is to beam upon us, our principle must be, that it is necessary to begin with heavenly teaching, and that it is impossible for any man to obtain even the minutest portion of right and sound doctrine without being a disciple of Scripture" (Calvin, Institutes, Bk. I, 6:2).

What has been said so far on the subject of Scripture has dealt primarily with its place in Protestant doctrine. What bearing does this fact have upon the place of Scripture in Christian apologetics? And what bearing does it have upon the method of apologetics in general? Anything approaching a full answer cannot be given till we come to discuss more particularly the relation of authority to reason in the following chapter. A few general remarks may be made here.

In the first place it must be affirmed that a Protestant accepts Scripture to be that which Scripture itself says it is on its own authority. Scripture presents itself as being the only light in terms of which the truth about facts and their relations can be discovered. Perhaps the relationship of the sun to our earth and the objects that constitute it, may make this clear. We do not use candles, or electric lights in order to discover whether the light and the energy of the sun exist. The reverse is the case. We have light in candles and electric light bulbs because of the light and energy of the sun. So we cannot subject the authoritative pronouncements of Scripture about reality to the scrutiny of reason because it is reason itself that learns its proper function from Scripture.

There are, no doubt, objections that occur to one at once when he hears the matter presented so baldly. Some of these will be taken up in the following chapter. For the moment it is of the greatest importance that this simple but basic point be considered apart from all subsidiary matters. All the objections that are brought against such a position spring, in the last analysis, from the assumption that the human person is ultimate and as such should properly act as judge of all claims to authority that are made by any one. But if man is not autonomous, if he is rather what Scripture says he is, namely, a creature of God and a sinner before his face, then man should subordinate his reason to the Scriptures and seek in the light of it to interpret his experience.

The proper attitude of reason to the authority of Scripture, then, is but typical of the proper attitude of reason to the whole of the revelation of God. The objects man must seek to know are always of such a nature as God asserts they are. God's revelation is always authoritarian. This is true of his revelation in nature no less than of his revelation in Scripture. The truly scientific method, the method which alone can expect to make true progress in learning, is therefore such a method as seeks simply to think God's thoughts after him.

When these matters are kept in mind, it will be seen clearly that the true method for any Protestant with respect to the Scripture (Christianity) and with respect to the existence of God (theism) must be the indirect method of reasoning by presupposition. In fact it then appears that the argument for the Scripture as the infallible revelation of God is, to all intents and purposes, the same as the argument for the existence of God. Protestants are required by the most basic principles of their system to vindicate the existence of no other God than the one who has spoken in the Scripture. But this God cannot be proved to exist by any other method than the indirect one of presupposition. No proof for this God and for the truth of his revelation in Scripture can be offered by an appeal to anything in human experience that has not itself received its light from the God whose existence and whose revelation it is supposed to prove. One cannot prove the usefulness of the light of the sun for the purposes of seeing by turning to the darkness of a cave. The darkness of the cave must itself be lit up by the shining of the sun. When the cave is thus lit up each of the objects that are in it "prove" the existence and character of the sun by receiving their light and intelligibility from it.

Now the Roman Catholic is not committed to any such doctrine of Scripture as has been expressed above. He can therefore build up his apologetics by the direct method. He can, as has already been shown, to a large extent agree with the natural man in his conception of both the starting point and the method of human knowledge. He can therefore join the non-Christian in his search for the existence or non-existence of God by the use of reason without any reference to Scripture. That is, he and the natural man can seek to build up theism quite independently of Christianity. Then when the Romanist has, together with his friend the natural man, built the first story of the house to the satisfaction of both, he will ask his friend to help in building the second story, the story of Christianity. He will assure his friend that he will use the same principles of construction for the second story that they have together employed in their common construction of the first story. The second story is, according to Rome, to be sure, the realm of faith and of authority. But then this authority is but that of the expert. Rome knows of no absolute authority such as Protestantism has in its doctrine of Scripture. Rome's authority is the authority of those who are experts in what they say are reported to be the oracles of God. These oracles receive their authoritative illumination from the expert interpreters of them, from the Pope first of all. But such a concept of authority resembles that which Socrates referred to in The Symposium when he spoke of Diotima the inspired. When the effort at rational interpretation failed him Socrates took refuge in mythology as a second best. The "hunch" of the wise is the best that is available to man with respect to that which he cannot reach by the methods of autonomous reason. No "wise man" ought to object to such a conception of the "supernatural." It merely involves the recognition that he has not yet discovered the truth about all of reality by means of reason. So then the natural man need not really object, even from his own point of view, to the presentation of supernatural revelation as it is offered to him by the Roman Catholic apologist.

If it be said here by way of objection that surely Roman Catholic theology is better than it is here presented as being, we readily admit this to be the case. But we maintain that if the Roman Catholic method of apologetic for Christianity is followed Christianity itself must be so reduced as to make it acceptable to the natural man. Since Rome is more than willing to grant the essential correctness of the starting point and method of the natural man in the "realm of nature" he cannot logically object to the conclusion of the natural man. The natural man need only to reason consistently along the lines of his starting point and method in order to reduce each of the Christian doctrines that are presented to him to naturalistic proportions.

As for the Arminian way of reasoning, it is, as already noted, essentially the same as that of Rome. The method followed by Bishop Butler follows closely that of Thomas Aquinas. According to Butler some of those who have no belief in or knowledge of Christianity at all have, none the less, quite rightly interpreted the "course and constitution of nature." The cave has already been lit up by means of light that has not derived from the sun. By the use of the empirical method those who make no pretense of listening to Scripture are said or assumed to have interpreted nature for what it really is. It is no wonder then that the contents of Scripture too must be adjusted to the likes of the natural man. He will not accept them otherwise. And Butler is anxious to win them. So he says to them: "Reason can, and it ought to judge, not only of the meaning, but also of the morality and the evidence, of revelation. First, it is the province of reason to judge of the morality of Scripture; i.e. not whether it contains things different from what we should have expected from a wise, just, and good Being; for objections from hence have now been obviated; but whether it contains things plainly contradictory to wisdom, justice, or goodness — to what the light of nature teaches us of God" (The Works of Bishop Butler, edited by Rt. Hon. W.E. Gladstone, Vol. I, p. 240). Since even in the interpretation of "nature" the natural man must and does himself admit that he cannot know everything, he can certainly without compromising himself in the least, allow that what the Scripture claims about "supernatural" things may probably be true. Already accustomed to allowing for a measure of discontinuity even in his interpretation of the "course and constitution of nature" why should he not allow for a little more of this same sort of discontinuity in realms about which he admits that he still may learn? Such a concession will not break the principle of continuity that he has employed in all his interpretations of things that he knows; his principle of continuity needs merely to be stretched. The natural man does not object to stretching his principle of continuity if he is compelled to do so by virtue of the irrationality of reality; the only thing to which he strenuously objects is the submission of his own principles of continuity and of discontinuity to the counsel of God.

It appears then that as Arminianism together with Roman Catholicism is willing to join the natural man in his supposedly neutral starting point and method, so also Arminianism is forced to pay for these concessions by having the natural man to some extent dictate to him what sort of Christianity he may or may not believe. If the natural man is given permission to draw the floor-plan for a house and is allowed to build the first story of the house in accordance with his own blueprint, the Christian cannot escape being controlled in a large measure by the same blueprint when he wants to take over the building of the second story of the house. Arminianism begins by offering to the natural man a Christian theology that has foreign elements in it. As over against the Reformed faith the Arminian has fought for the idea of man's ultimate ability to accept or reject salvation. His argument on this score amounts to saying that God's presentation of his claims upon mankind cannot reach down to the individual man; it can only reach to the infima species. God has to await the election returns to see whether he is chosen as God or is set aside. God's knowledge therefore stands over against and depends to some extent upon a temporal reality which he does not wholly control. When the Arminian has thus, as he thinks, established and defended human responsibility against the Calvinist he turns about to defend the Christian position against the natural man. But then he soon finds himself at the mercy of the natural man. The natural man is mercilessly consistent. He simply tells the Arminian that a little autonomy involves absolute autonomy, and a little reality set free from the plan of God involves all reality set free from the plan of God. After that the reduction process is simply a matter of time. Each time the Arminian presents to the natural man one of the doctrines of Christianity, the natural man gladly accepts it and then "natural-izes" it.

It is no valid objection against this contention to say that certainly many Arminians do not hold to any naturalistic conception of Christianity. For the question is not so much now what individual Arminians believe. Their belief at best involves a compromise with naturalism. But the point we are making now is about the method of apologetics that fits in with Arminian theology. And on that score we must, in simple honesty, assert that this method is essentially the same as the method of Roman Catholicism and is essentially reductionistic and therefore self-frustrative. It appears then that the first enemy of Arminianism, namely Calvinism, is its best friend. Only in the Reformed Faith is there an uncompromising statement of the main tenets of Christianity. All other statements are deformations. It is but to be expected that only in the Reformed Faith will we find an uncompromising method of apologetics. Calvinism makes no compromise with the natural man either on his views of the autonomy of the human mind or on his views of the nature of existence as not controlled by the plan of God. Therefore Calvinism cannot find a direct point of contact in any of the accepted concepts of the natural man. He disagrees with every individual doctrine of the natural man because he disagrees with the outlook of the natural man as a whole. He disagrees with the basic immanentistic assumption of the natural man. For it is this basic assumption that colors all his statements about individual teachings. It is therefore this basic assumption of the natural man that meets its first major challenge when it is confronted by the statement of a full-fledged Christianity.

The Reformed apologist throws down the gauntlet and challenges his opponent to a duel of life and death from the start. He does not first travel in the same direction and in the same automobile with the natural man for some distance in order then mildly to suggest to the driver that they ought perhaps to change their course somewhat and follow a road that goes at a different slant from the one they are on. The Reformed apologist knows that there is but one way to the truth and that the natural man is travelling it, but in the wrong direction. The service stations along the highway will service cars going in either direction. And as there are more cars going in the wrong direction than there are going in the right direction, the upkeep of the road will be supplied largely by those going in the wrong direction. Speaking together at one of these service stations, two travelers going in opposite directions may be in perfect agreement when they eulogize the turnpike on which they are traveling and the premium quality of Sunoco gasoline which they are getting without paying a premium price. But like Bunyan's Christian, the Reformed apologist will tell his friend that the way he is going leads to the precipice. He points to the signs made by the builder of the road which all point the opposite way from that which his friend, the natural man, is going. And when the reply is made by the natural man that he has been very successful in his trip so far, and that he too has been following

71

signs, signs which point in the direction in which he is moving, the Reformed apologist will wipe out such of these signs as are near at hand and will challenge his friend to wipe out any of the signs he has ignored.

The Roman Catholic and the Arminian apologist would not be in a position to wipe out any of the signs that point in the wrong direction. An Arminian apologist meeting the natural man as both stop at one of the service stations is in a strange predicament. Since he is a Christian he should really speak to the natural man about the fact that he is following the wrong signs. His belief in creation demands of him that he warn his new acquaintance against following the wrong signs. But since he himself holds to a measure of autonomy for man and since this undermines his own belief in creation, he can at best say to his friend that it is doubtful which signs are right. Then as far as his "neutral" apologetic method is concerned, the Arminian, in the interest of getting his friend to go in the right direction, admits that the signs that point in the wrong direction are right. He himself goes in the wrong direction for some distance too with the natural man. He fully agrees with the natural man when together they start on their wrong course and he still fully agrees on the way to the city of destruction. Then suddenly he puts on the brakes and turns around expecting that his friend will do the same. Thus in the whole business he has dishonored his God (a) by practically admitting that his revelation is not plain, and (b) by himself running away from God in his interpretation of natural revelation and his subjection of supernatural revelation to the illegitimate requirements of the natural man. Meanwhile he has failed in his purpose of persuading the natural man to go in the right direction. The Roman Catholic and Arminian views of theology are compromising; in consequence, the Roman Catholic and the Arminian method of apologetics is both compromising and self-frustrative.

Block-house Methodology

A final point must be made before concluding this chapter. We have seen that the proper method for Protestant apologetics is that of presupposition instead of the direct approach. But the theology of Rome and the theology of Arminianism does not permit such an argument. Roman Catholics and Arminians must of necessity argue by way of direct approach. As deformations of Christian theism they contain no challenge to the position of the natural man till it is too late.

We have also seen that the method of presupposition requires the presentation of Christian theism as a unit. But the theology of Roman Catholics compels them to deal with theism first and with Christianity afterwards. Assigning to reason the task of interpreting nature without dependence upon Scripture, this theology is bound to prove the truth of theism first. The theism that is proved in this way cannot be the only theism that any Christian should want to prove, namely, Christian theism. Yet having proved some sort of theism by "reason," the Roman Catholic is bound by virtue of his theology to prove a type of Christianity that will fit on to the deformation of theism it has "established." And what holds true of Roman Catholicism holds true fundamentally also of Arminianism.

It remains now to indicate more fully than has been done that the Roman Catholic and Arminian method of reasoning is bound, not merely to cut the unity of Christian theism in two, but is bound even to prove its theism piece by piece. Romanism and Arminianism lead not merely to dualism but to atomism in methodology.

A truly Protestant method of reasoning involves a stress upon the fact that the meaning of every aspect or part of Christian theism depends upon Christian theism as a unit. When Protestants speak of the resurrection of Christ they speak of the resurrection of him who is the Son of God, the eternal Word through whom the world was made. The truth of theism is involved in this claim that Christians make with respect to the domain of history. And what is true of the resurrection of Christ is true with respect to all the propositions about historical fact that are made in Scripture. No proposition about historical fact is presented for what it really is till it is presented as a part of the system of Christian theism that is contained in Scripture. To say this is involved in the consideration that all facts of the created universe are what they are by virtue of the plan of God with respect to them. Any fact in any realm confronted by man is what it is as revelational through and through of the God and of the Christ of Christian theism.

But if this is true — and it would seem to be of the very essence of the biblical point of view to say that it is true — then it follows that the whole claim of Christian theism is in question in any debate about any fact. Christian theism must be presented as that light in terms of which any proposition about any fact receives meaning. Without the presupposition of the truth of Christian theism no fact can be distinguished from any other fact. To say this is but to apply the method of idealist logicians in a way that these idealist logicians, because of their own anti-Christian theistic assumptions, cannot apply it. The point made by these logicians is that even the mere counting of particular things presupposes a system of truth of which these particulars form a part. Without such a system of truth there would be no distinguishable difference between one particular and another. They would be as impossible to distinguish from one another as the millions of drops of water in the ocean would be indistinguishable from one another by the naked eye. "The main point is this, that all counting presupposes and depends upon a qualitative whole, and that the Collective Judgment asserts a generic connection within its group. Hence no more particulars can be counted" (F.H. Bradley, The Principles of Logic, Vol. I, page 369).

It may be objected that one fact differs from other facts precisely because none of them are rationally controlled. Is it not the insertion of individual facts into a logically concatenated system that makes these facts lose their individuality? Has not Kant taught us that, if we are to have logical concatenation between the individual facts of our experience at all, we can have it just to the extent that we give up the impossible ideal of knowing individual things in themselves?

In reply we need only to observe that this way of escape is not open to the Reformed apologist. The Reformed apologist must, if he is at the same time a Reformed theologian, hold to what the average scientist and philosopher today will look upon as the most hopeless form of rationalism he has ever met. The historical forms of rationalism have done either of two things. If they were reasonably consistent then they were ready to deny the existence and meaning of individuality in history altogether. Parmenides claimed that the "great question, Is it or is it not?" was to be determined by what man can consistently say about it (Burnet, Greek Philosophy Part I, Thales to Plato, p. 67). This was consistent rationalism. Parmenides was therefore ready to assert the non-existence and meaninglessness of individual historical factuality. On the other hand, if rationalists were consistent they held to the same ideal of individuation by means of complete logical description on the part of man but they realized that such a description cannot be accomplished. Leibniz was not less a rationalist in his hopes and ambitions than was Parmenides. He does not hesitate to make the "possibility of knowledge to depend upon a knowledge of possibility." Yet, Leibniz questions whether man can ever attain to the perfect analysis, which would carry him back, without finding any contradiction, to the absolute attributes of God. (Martin, Clark, Clarke, Rudick A History of Philosophy, p. 396). Thus, in spite of himself, Leibniz has to allow for the actual existence of individual, ultimately changing things. But then to do so he has to sacrifice his system of logic. He recognizes temporal individuality but can do so only at the expense of logical system. Thus the rationalist agrees with the irrationalist that individuality in fact can exist only at the expense of logical system. And the idealist logicians, such as F.H. Bradley and Bernard Bosanquet are no exceptions to this rule. But in contradistinction from the rationalist and the irrationalist, and in contradistinction from the forms of thought that seek some sort of combination between these two, the Reformed apologist must hold both to the idea of absolute system and to that of genuine historic fact and individuality. He does not hold to "truths of fact" at the expense of "truths of reason." He holds to truths of fact only because to him they are truths of reason. But then it is obvious that he is not himself, as a human being, able to show the exhaustive logical relationships between the facts of history and nature which are in debate as between believers and disbelievers in Christian theism. In consequence he must maintain that the truths of fact presented in Scripture must be what Scripture says they are or else they are irrational and meaningless altogether. The true Christian apologist has his principle of discontinuity; it is expressed in his appeal to the mind of God as all-comprehensive in knowledge because all-controlling in power. He holds his principle of discontinuity then, not at the expense of all logical relationship between facts, but because of the recognition of his creaturehood. His principle of discontinuity is therefore the opposite of that of irrationalism without being that of rationalism. The Christian also has his principle of continuity. It is that of the self-contained God and his plan for history. His principle of continuity is therefore the opposite of that of rationalism without being that of irrationalism.

Conjoining the Christian principle of continuity and the Christian principle of discontinuity we obtain the Christian principle of reasoning by presupposition. It is the actual existence of the God of Christian theism and the infallible authority of the Scripture which speaks to sinners of this God that must be taken as the presupposition of the intelligibility of any fact in the world.

This does not imply that it will be possible to bring the whole debate about Christian theism to full expression in every discussion of individual historical fact. Nor does it imply that the debate about historical detail is unimportant. It means that no Christian apologist can afford to forget the claim of his system with respect to any particular fact. He must always maintain that the "fact" under discussion with his opponent must be what Scripture says it is, if it is to be intelligible as a fact at all. He must maintain that there can be no facts in any realm but such as actually do exhibit the truth of the system of which they are a part. If facts are what they are as parts of the Christian theistic system of truth then what else can facts do but reveal that system to the limit of their ability as parts of that system? It is only as manifestations of that system that they are what they are. If the apologist does not present them as such he does not present them for what they are.

Over against this Christian theistic position, any non-Christian philosophy virtually denies the unity of truth. It may speak much of it and even seem to contend for it, as idealistic philosophers do, but in the last analysis non-Christian philosophy is atomistic. This follows from the absolute separation between truth and reality that was introduced when Adam and Eve fell away from God. When Satan tempted Eve to eat of the forbidden fruit he tried to persuade her that God's announcement of the consequences of such an act would not come true. That was tantamount to saying that no assertion about a rational scheme could predict the course of movement of time-controlled reality. Reality, Satan practically urged man, was to be conceived of as something that is not under rational control. Every non-Christian philosophy makes the assumption made by Adam and Eve, and is therefore irrationalistic. This irrationalism comes to most consistent expression in various forms of empiricism and pragmatism. In them predication is frankly conceived of in atomistic fashion.

On the other hand when Satan tempted Eve he virtually asked her to become a rationalist. He asked her to take the position that she needed not to obtain any information about the course of factual eventuation from any source but her own mind. Prior to any tendency that had developed in the course of historical events she, following Satan's advice, made what was tantamount to a universal negative judgment about time reality. She took for granted that punishment could not come in consequence upon her eating of the forbidden fruit. This rationalism appears most consistently in such men as Parmenides. But even the inconsistent rationalists are really a priorists; they make concessions only because they cannot realize their ideal. "The rationalists (Descartes, Spinoza and Leibniz) argued that all knowledge comes from reason alone" (G.H.C. in Christian Opinion, Jan. 1945). Yet Leibniz was forced to speak of truths of fact as well as of truths of reason.

In modern times Kant has combined the principles of rationalism and empiricism. "He described the contribution of reason to knowledge as exactly so and so and the contribution of sense as exactly such and such" (G. H.C. ibid). This position of Kant is the dominating position that confronts us today. It is usually spoken of as phenomenalistic. It is characterized by an attempt to bridge the gulf between fact and mind that was brought into the world as the consequence of the sin of Adam. But it cannot be a remedy for this dualism. Phenomenalism is still basically atomistic inasmuch as it still maintains that factuality in itself is non-rational in character. At the same time phenomenalism is still rationalistic in that whatever of unity it thinks it finds in this atomistically conceived reality virtually proceeds from the human mind. At least this rationality is not taken as proceeding from the mind of God. The rationalizing effort that is inherent in phenomenalism would, if successful, destroy all individuality. Its rationalizing effort is admittedly a step by step affair. That this is so is evident from the fact that its rationalizations are rationalizations of admittedly non-rational material. Phenomenalism builds up its island of rationality by taking dirt from its center and patching it on to its side, much as the Chicago lake front was built up gradually with dirt hauled into the water from the land. The difference is that the phenomenalists have no right to think of a bottom underneath the water into which they throw their dirt.

The dilemma that confronts the non-Christian methodology in general, and that of modern phenomenalism in particular, is therefore that one must either know everything or one cannot know anything. One assumption is that unless one knows the terms or objects of propositions in the fulness of their relationships one does not know them at all. A second assumption is that the terms of propositions are not merely unknown but ultimately unknowable in all their relationships. And what is called scientific knowledge is a cross between knowing everything about nothing and knowing nothing about "everything." "A completed rational system having nothing outside of it nor any possible alternative to it, is both presupposed and beyond the actual attainment of any one moment" (Cohen, Reason and Nature, p. 158).

The point we are now concerned to stress is the atomistic character of the non-Christian methodology. The idea of system is for it merely a limiting notion. It is merely an ideal. What is more, it must forever remain but an ideal. To become a reality this ideal would have to destroy science itself. It would have to demolish the individuality of each fact as it came to know it. But if it did this, it would no longer be knowledge of a fact that is different from any other fact. The method of non-Christian science then requires that to be known facts must be known as part of a system. And since the Christian idea of system as due to the counsel of God is by definition excluded, it is man himself that must know this system. But to know the system he must know it intuitively. He cannot know it discursively because discursive thought, if it is to be in contact with reality at all, must partake of the piecemeal character of non-rational being. Each individual concept that pretends to be a concept with respect to things that have their existence in the world of time must partake of the de facto character of these facts themselves. In consequence each judgment or each proposition that is made by discursive thought about temporal existence is also characterized by the de facto character of temporal existence itself. Each proposition then, as far as all practical purposes are concerned would have to be thought of as standing essentially by itself and as intelligible by itself. There could be no logically necessary connection between the various judgments of discursive thought; there could be only an intuition that as F.H. Bradley put it, somehow Reality contains the harmony that is not found in appearance.

If at this point the idea of God is introduced and it is said that while man of necessity cannot know otherwise than discursively and therefore cannot know all things, but that God knows intuitively and therefore does know all things, the reply would be that such a God must then stand in a non-rational relation to the universe and to the knowledge which man possesses. Always bound to think atomistically man could know nothing of a God who knows intuitively and yet knows individuality and concrete historical factuality. Aristotle's God is just such a God. To the extent that he knows intuitively he knows nothing of individual existence. He knows himself and men only to the extent that they are exhaustively classified and when they are so classified and he therefore knows them, he does not know them. And Aristotle's man knows nothing of Aristotle's God.

It is not difficult to see that the Christian position requires the apologist to challenge this whole approach in the interest of the knowledge of the truth. If man's necessarily discursive thought is not to fall into the ultimate irrationalism and scepticism that is involved in modern methodology we must presuppose the conception of the God that is found in Scripture. Scripture alone presents the sort of God whose intuition of system is not bought at the price of his knowledge of individuality, and whose knowledge of individuality is not bought at the expense of intuitional knowledge of system. But such a God must really be presupposed. He must be taken as the prerequisite of the possibility and actuality of relationship between man's various concepts and propositions of knowledge. Man's system of knowledge must therefore be an anological replica of the system of knowledge which belongs to God.

We need not now pursue this matter further. It must rather be pointed out in this connection that since Roman Catholicism and Arminianism are committed to a neutral starting point and methodology they are bound also to fall into the atomism of non-Christian thought. Since they will not look at all the facts as facts of the Christian theistic system, and flatly refuse to admit that anything but a Christian theistic fact can exist at all, and with this claim challenge the non-Christian methodology from the outset of the argument, they are bound to be carried away to a non-Christian conclusion. It is of the essence of both the Romanist and the Arminian method of argumentation to agree with the non-Christian that individual propositions about many dimensions of reality are true whether Christianity is true or not. Neither Roman Catholics nor Arminian apologists are in a position to challenge the natural man's atomistic procedure. Their own theologies are atomistic. They are not built along consistently Christian lines. Their individual doctrines are therefore not presented as being what they are exclusively by virtue of their relation to the main principles of the Christian position. Their contention that the Reformed faith is wrong in thinking of all things in the world as being what they are ultimately in virtue of God's plan with respect to them compels the Roman Catholic and the Arminian apologist to admit the essential correctness of non-Christian atomism. And herewith they have at the same time lost all power to challenge the non-Christian methodology at the outset of its career. Instead they themselves become the victims of this method. Since the principles of their theology will not permit them to argue by way of presupposition, their own piece-meal presentation of Christian theism constantly comes to a sorry end. It is as though an army were sending out a few individual soldiers in order to wrest some atoll from a powerful concentration of an enemy's forces. There can be no joining of issues at the central point of difference, the interpretation by exclusively immanentistic categories or the interpretation in terms of the self-sufficient God, unless it be done by way of presupposition. And the Reformed apologist has a theology that both permits and requires him to do this.

CHAPTER V

AUTHORITY AND REASON

The general principles of methodology that have been discussed in the preceding chapter must now be applied to the problem of authority. Here, if anywhere, the difference between the Protestant and the Roman Catholic methodology becomes clearly apparent. For Rome the authority of the church, in particular that of the Pope, speaking ex cathedra is ultimate; for Protestantism the Scripture stands above every statement of the church and its teachers.

The question that now confronts us is as to how the Roman Catholic and how the Protestant approaches the non-believer on the question of authority.

To answer this question it is well that we begin by asking what place the non-believer himself attributes to authority. And in order to discover the place allowed to authority by the natural man it is imperative to note what he means by authority.

There are those, of course, who deny that they need any form of authority. They are the popular atheists and agnostics. Such men say that they must be shown by "reason" whatever they are to accept as true. But the great thinkers among non-Christian men have taken no such position. They know that they cannot cover the whole area of reality with their knowledge. They are therefore willing to admit that there may be others who have information that they themselves do not possess. In everyday life this sort of thing is illustrated in the idea of the expert. A medical doctor knows much about the human body that the rest of us do not know. Then among medical men there are those who, because of natural ability, industry and opportunity make such discoveries as their fellows do not make. So everywhere and in all respects the lesser minds are bound to submit to the authority of greater minds.

In putting the matter in this way the nature of the authority that can be allowed by the natural man is already indicated. The natural man will gladly allow for the idea of authority if only it be the authority of the expert in the use of reason. Such a conception of authority is quite consistent with the assumption of the sinner's autonomy.

On the other hand the conception of authority as something that stands "above reason" is unacceptable to the natural man. But it is not easy to distinguish in every instance when authority is considered to be "above reason." There are some forms of authority that might seem, at first sight, to be "above reason" while in reality they are not. Some discussion of this matter must therefore precede our analysis of the difference between the Roman Catholic and the Protestant methods of presenting the authority of Christianity to the natural man.

Let us note then some of the forms of authority that are quite acceptable to the natural man because, to his mind, they do not violate the principle of autonomy.

First there is the need for authority that grows out of the existence of the endless multiplicity of factual material. Time rolls its ceaseless course. It pours out upon us an endless stream of facts. And the stream is really endless on the non-Christian basis. For those who do not believe that all that happens in time happens because of the plan of God, the activity of time is like to that, or rather is identical with that, of Chance. Thus the ocean of facts has no bottom and no shore. It is this conception of the ultimacy of time and of pure factuality on which modern philosophy, particularly since the days of Kant, has laid such great stress. And it is because of the general recognition of the ultimacy of chance that rationalism of the sort that Descartes, Spinoza and Leibniz represented, is out of date. It has become customary to speak of post-Kantian philosophy as irrationalistic. It has been said that Kant limited reason so as to make room for faith. Hence there are those who are willing to grant that man's emotions or his will can get in touch with such aspects of reality as are not accessible to the intellect. The intellect, it is said, is not the only, and in religious matters not even the primary instrument, with which men come into contact with what is ultimate in human experience. There is the world of the moral imperative, of aesthetic appreciation, of the religious a priori as well as the world of science. There is in short the world of "mystery" into which the prophet or genius of feeling or of will may lead us.

It is of the greatest import to note that the natural man need not in the least object to the kind of authority that is involved in the idea of irrationalism. And that chiefly for two reasons. In the first place the irrationalism of our day is the direct lineal descendant of the rationalism of previous days. The idea of pure chance has been inherent in every form of non-Christian thought in the past. It is the only logical alternative to the position of Christianity according to which the plan of God is back of all. Both Plato and Aristotle were compelled to make room for it in their maturest thought. The pure "not-being" of the earliest rationalism of Greece was but the suppressed "otherness" of the final philosophy of Plato. So too the idea of pure factuality or pure chance as ultimate is but the idea of "otherness" made explicit. Given the non-Christian assumption with respect to man's autonomy the idea of chance has equal rights with the idea of logic. If Parmenides was first upon the scene to press the claims of the intellect by saying that to be and to know ought for man to be coterminous, it was natural that chance would not fail at some time in the future to assert its independence.

In the second place modern irrationalism has not in the least encroached upon the domain of the intellect as the natural man thinks of it. Irrationalism has merely taken possession of that which the intellect, by its own admission, cannot in any case control. Irrationalism has a secret treaty with rationalism by which the former cedes to the latter so much of its territory as the latter can at any given time find the forces to control. Kant's realm of the noumenal has, as it were, agreed to yield so much of its area to the phenomenal, as the intellect by its newest weapons can manage to keep in control. Moreoever, by the same treaty irrationalism has promised to keep out of its own territory any form of authority that might be objectionable to the autonomous intellect. The very idea of pure factuality or chance is the best guarantee that no true authority, such as that of God as the Creator and Judge of men, will ever confront man. If we compare the realm of the phenomenal as it has been ordered by the autonomous intellect to a clearing in a large forest we may compare the realm of the noumenal to that part of the same forest which has not yet been laid under contribution by the intellect. The realm of mystery is on this basis simply the realm of that which is not yet known. And the service of irrationalism to rationalism may be compared to that of some bold huntsman in the woods who keeps all lions and tigers away from the clearing. This bold huntsman covers the whole of the infinitely extended forest ever keeping away all danger from the clearing. This irrationalistic Robin Hood is so much of a rationalist that he virtually makes a universal negative statement about what <u>can</u> happen in all future time. In the secret treaty spoken of he has assured the intellect of the autonomous man that the God of Christianity cannot possibly exist and that no man therefore need to fear the coming of a judgment. If the whole course of history is, at least in part, controlled by chance, then there is no danger that the autonomous man will ever meet with the claims of authority as the Protestant believes in it. For the notion of authority is but the expression of the idea that God by his counsel controls all things that happen in the course of history.

There is a second kind of authority that the natural man is quite ready to accept. It does not spring as did the first, from the fact that the intellect can by definition not control the whole realm of chance. It springs from the fact that even that which the intellect does assert about the objects of knowledge is, of necessity involved in contradiction. F.H. Bradley's great book, <u>Appearance</u> and <u>Reality</u>, has brought out this point with the greatest possible detail. The point is not that the many philosophers who have speculated on the nature of reality have actually contradicted each other and themselves. The point is rather that in the nature of the case all logical assertion with respect to the world of temporal existence must needs be self-contradictory in character.

On the assumptions of the natural man logic is a timeless impersonal principle, as factuality is controlled by chance. It is by means of universal timeless principles of logic that the natural man must, on his assumptions,

seek to make intelligible assertions about the world of reality or chance.
But this cannot be done without falling into self-contradiction. About chance
no manner of assertion can be made. In its very idea it is the irrational.
And how are rational assertions to be made about the irrational? If they are
to be made then it must be because the irrational is itself wholly reduced to
the rational. That is to say if the natural man is to make any intelligible
assertions about the world of "reality" or "fact" which, according to him
is what it is for no rational reason at all, then he must make the virtual
claim of rationalizing the irrational. To be able to distinguish one fact from
another fact he must reduce all time existence, all factuality to immovable
timeless being. But when he has done so he has killed all individuality and
factuality as conceived of on his basis. Thus the natural man must on the
one hand assert that all reality is non-structural in nature and on the other
hand that all reality is structural in nature. He must even assert on the one
hand that all reality is non-structurable in nature and on the other hand that
he himself has virtually structured all of it. Thus all his predication is in
the nature of the case self-contradictory.

Realizing this dilemma, many modern philosophers have argued that
any intellectual system of interpretation is therefore no more than a perspective. No system, these men assert, should pretend to be more than a
system "for us." We have to deal with reality as if it will always behave
as we have found it behaving in the past. The world of appearance formed
by means of the exercise of the intellect must be taken as "somehow" similar to the world of Reality. And thus we seem to have come again upon the
idea of mystery, the world of "faith" and of "authority" where prophets
and seers may suggest to us the visions they have seen in the night.

Such then seems to be the present situation. Modern philosophy in
practically all of its schools admits that all its speculations end in mystery.
Speaking generally, modern philosophy (and science) is phenomenalistic. It
admits that ultimate reality is unknowable to man. All systems of interpretation are said to be necessarily relative to the mind of man. And so it
seems at first sight that modern philosophy ought, on its own principles, to
admit that there is a dimension of reality that is beyond its reach and about
which it ought therefore to be ready to listen by the avenue of authority.
Modern philosophy would seem to be ready therefore to listen to the voice
of "religion." So for instance Dorothy Emmet views the matter. "The
heart of religion, as far as I can see it, seems to be an intuitive response
to something which evokes worship. Let me first explain what I mean by
'intuitive.' I am using the word to mean a kind of apprehension which is
reached by methods other than those of critical reflection. It is the kind of
reflection we use when we grasp the character of a person, or the demands
of a situation, without being aware of the steps by which we have arrived at
our judgment" (Philosophy and Faith, London, 1936, p. 84). On such a view
it might seem that one should be able to accept the authority of Jesus. And
Miss Emmet can allow for the authority of Jesus. But it is still no more

than the authority of the expert. For those who think as she does, Jesus is nothing more than the kind of person they would like to be and could be if only they lived up to their own ideals.

The natural man then assumes that he has the final criterion of truth within himself. Every form of authority that comes to him must justify itself by standards inherent in man and operative apart from the authority that speaks.

But what has been said has dealt only with modern philosophy. A word must be added about modern theology. Surely we shall find here a more ready recognition of the need of authority! More than that we shall expect to find here the advocates of authority! But in this we are disappointed. Modern theology is, to be sure, ready to defend the need and place of authority. But it will defend no authority that is not acceptable to modern philosophy and science. It too advocates the authority of the expert only.

It needs no argument to prove this contention true with respect to Schleiermacher, the father of modern theology. His great work The Christian Faith is largely controlled in its epistemology by the principles of Kant's Critique of Pure Reason. He speaks, to be sure, of the religious man and of his absolute dependence upon God. He seems to limit the claims of the human intellect. He says that by means of it we cannot reach God. It is by our feeling of dependence that we have contact with God. But in all this he is simply setting forth a religious phenomenalism. It is no virtue to decry the autonomous intellect if one sets up in its stead an autonomous feeling. And that is precisely what Schleiermacher does. In his theology it is still the human personality as such that has the final criterion of truth within itself.

For a contemporary discussion of the relation between authority and reason on the part of a great churchman and a great philosopher we may turn to the work of A.E. Taylor, The Faith of a Moralist. Taylor pleads for a place for authority in human thought. But no authority, he says, can be absolute. An absolute authority could not be transmitted through history, and if it could be transmitted it could not be received. The mind of man contributes to all that it receives. Kant has taught us this once for all and we cannot depart from it. Hence no orthodox doctrine of authority can ever be accepted. Such is the burden of Taylor's argument and it is typical of what one hears in varying forms (Vol. II, p. 200 ff.).

The late archbishop William Temple also asks for no higher authority than that of the expert in his work Nature, Man and God, London, 1925. The spiritual authority of revelation, he contends, "depends wholly upon the spiritual quality of what is revealed" (p. 347). And whether what is revealed be spiritual, of that, argues Temple in effect, man himself must ever be the final judge.

But what of Karl Barth and Emil Brunner? Have they not bravely contended for the "absolutely other" God? Are not they the "theologians of the Word"? Look at the lashing Barth gives the "consciousness theologians," the followers of Schleiermacher and Ritschl, just because they have been virtual ventriloquists, speaking in the name of God that which in reality proceeds only from themselves (Dogmatik, 1927). Note too with what increasing consistency through the periods of his development Barth has set his theology over against that of "modern Protestantism." A true theology, argues Barth, has its chief canon in the first commandment, "Thou shalt have no other gods before me" instead of in the logic of Aristotle or Kant. A true theology must break with all systems of philosophy, with all the promethean constructions of the human intellect and reach man in the depth of his being with the voice of God's authority speaking in its own name. Here then it would seem that among all the "types of modern theology" we have found one that stands up like a Daniel against modern philosophy and science with the voice of the living God.

Sad to say, however, the "absolutely other" God of Barth is absolutely other only in the way that a sky-rocket is "absolutely other" to the mind of the child. Barth's god has first been cast up into the heights by the projective activity of the would-be autonomous man. In all his thinking Barth is, in spite of his efforts to escape it, still controlled by some form of modern critical philosophy. And this means that the mind of man is always thought of as contributing something ultimate to all the information it has and receives. Accordingly the "absolutely other" god of Barth remains absolute just so long as he is absolutely unknown. In that case he is identical with the realm of mystery which the autonomous man admits of as existing beyond the reach of its thought. It then has no more content and significance than the vaguest conception of something indeterminate. There is no more meaning in the idea of God as Barth holds it than there was in the idea of the apeiron, the indefinite, of Anaximander the Greek philosopher. On the other hand when the god of Barth does reveal himself he reveals himself wholly. For Barth God is exhaustively known if he is known at all. That is to say to the extent that this god is known he is nothing distinct from the principles that are operative in the universe. He is then wholly identical with man and his world. It appears then that when the god of Barth is wholly mysterious and as such should manifest himself by revelation only, he remains wholly mysterious and does not reveal himself. On the other hand when this god does reveal himself his revelation is identical with what man can know apart from such a revelation. Thus there is absolute authority which either says nothing or when it says something has lost its character as authority. And the fact that Barth thinks of revelation dialectically means in this connection only that his god is both absolutely hidden and absolutely revealed simultaneously. And this can be maintained only if the very idea of authority as orthodox Christianity conceives of it on the basis of the Creator creature distinction has first been discarded. If this distinction is maintained there can be no such dialectical relationship between the hidden and the revealed character of

God. In that case God cannot, to be sure, ever reveal himself exhaustively. The mind of man is finite and knows only by thinking God's thoughts after him. But what it knows it then knows truly. It has at its disposal the revelation of God. This revelation does not hide God while it reveals him; it reveals him truly, though not exhaustively.

What has been said about Barth holds, with minor changes, also for Emil Brunner and for such other theologians as Reinhold Niehbuhr, Richard Niehbuhr, Nels R. Feree, John A. Mackay and Elmer George Homrighausen. In their theology, as in that of Barth, it is the autonomous religious consciousness that divides itself into two sections after the style of Dr. Jekyll and Mr. Hyde. The higher aspect addresses itself to the lower aspect and insists upon obedience to its voice. Thus men tell themselves that they have listened to and obeyed the voice of Jesus or of God, while they have only obeyed themselves.

It appears then that, in Protestant circles at least, there seems in our day to be general agreement as to the nature of authority and the relation it is to sustain to reason. There is a quite general acceptance of authority but it is merely the authority of the expert. And this authority presupposes that, in the last analysis, man is dealing with an ultimately mysterious environment. It takes for granted that God, no less than man, is surrounded by mystery. It is no wonder that those who work on the principle of the autonomy of reason have no difficulty in accepting such a concept of authority. The followers of the autonomous reason have, in modern times, themselves asserted the need of the idea of the ultimately mysterious. The Mysterious Universe, the universe in which facts are what they are for no rational reason, is the presupposition both of modern science and of modern philosophy. And this position is not challenged by modern theology.

Is it then to the church of Rome that we must go in order to find a challenge to this modern concept of reason as autonomous, and of authority as merely that of those who have probed the realm of utter darkness a little more deeply than others? At first sight this might seem to be the case. A. E. Taylor relates a little story that might seem to point in that direction. "It relates," he says, "that a Roman Catholic theologian was in conversation with an outsider, who remarked that there seemed to be no real difference between the position of Rome and that of a well-known and highly respected 'Anglo-Catholic.' 'Pardon me,' replied the theologian, 'we are at the opposite pole from X. He holds every doctrine we hold, but holds them for the entirely irrelevant reason that he thinks them true' " (The Faith of a Moralist, Vol. II, p. 198). But this story in and by itself would not give an adequate notion of the Roman Catholic position either on the meaning of authority or on its relation to reason. A brief word must therefore be said on the subject.

To ascertain the Romish concept of reason, we may start from the fact that by Roman Catholic theologians Aristotle is taken to be the "philosopher par excellence, as St. Thomas is the theologian" (J. Maritain, An Introduction to Philosophy, 1937, p. 99). Now theology, says Maritain, presupposes certain truths of the "natural order." These truths are naturally known to all men and are worked out scientifically by the philosophers and particularly by Aristotle. The "premises of philosophy are self-supported and are not derived from those of theology" (Idem, p. 126). Ettienne Gilson expresses the same thought when he says: "The heritage of Greek thought, even when cut to the minimum and judged most critically, is still worthy of admiration. So true is this that a number of the Fathers were convinced that the pagan thinkers had access to the Bible without admitting it. One first being, the supreme cause and principle and cause of nature, source of all intelligibility, of all order, and of all beauty, who eternally leads a life of happiness, because, being thought itself, it is an eternal contemplation of its own thought, all that was taught by Aristotle; and if we compare his theology to the ancient mythologies we will see at a glance what immense progress human reason had made since the era of Chronos and Jupiter without the aid of Christian Revelation. Doubtless there were many lacunae, and numberless errors mingled with these truths. But they were still truths. Discovered by the natural reason of the Greeks, they owed nothing to faith; still discoverable today, with even greater ease, by the same natural reason, why should they owe more to faith in our own reason than in Aristotle's?" (Christianity and Philosophy, 1939).

Besides this "natural order" which can be discovered by reason apart from faith, there is the order of faith. And as the assertions by reason in the natural order do not depend for their validity upon faith, so those in the order of faith do not depend for their validity upon the assertions of reason. "The affirmations of Catholic faith ultimately depend on no reasoning, fallible or otherwise, but on the Word of God. For indeed whatever reason is able to know about God with a perfect knowledge, precisely because it is thus knowable, cannot essentially belong in the order of faith" (Idem, p. 56).

The order of nature as set forth by autonomous reason and the order of faith accepted exclusively on authority both deal with God and his relation to man. The question that at once appears is as to how it may be known that the God of reason and the God of faith are the same God. There is the more reason for asking this question inasmuch as it is admitted that the reason which discovers the truths of the natural order is "wounded." "The true Catholic position consists in maintaining that nature was created good, that it had been wounded, but that it can be at least partially healed by grace if God so wishes" (Idem, p. 21). It might seem that grace must first restore the powers of reason at least to the extent of healing its wounds before reason can function normally. And Gilson does in fact speak of a Christian philosophy which is the product of a reason that is restored by grace. Such a philosophy, he argues, is the best philosophy. It is the best philosophy because in it reason best comes to its own. But even so the problem remains the same. Here it is Aristotle who has by means of his wounded reason constructed the truths of the natural order as noted. Is then the God whom Aristotle discovers the same God of whom Christian theology speaks?

Gilson himself confronts us with the seriousness of the problem when he says in pointed fashion that reason or philosophy can deal only with essences and not with existence. Yet it is of the existence of God that it is supposed to speak.

"When, for instance, Aristotle was positing his first self-thinking Thought as the supreme being, he certainly conceived it as pure Act and as an infinitely powerful energy; still, his god was but the pure Act of a Thought. This infinitely powerful actuality of a self-thinking principle most certainly deserves to be called pure Act, but it was a pure Act in the order of knowing, not in that of existence. Now nothing can give it what it has not. Because the supreme Thought of Aristotle was not 'He who is,' it could not give existence: hence the world of Aristotle was not a created world. Because the supreme Thought of Aristotle was not the pure Act of existing, its self-knowledge did not entail the knowledge of all being, both actual and possible: the god of Aristotle was not a providence; he did not even know a world which he did not make and which he could not possibly have made because he was the thought of a Thought, nor did he know the self-awareness of 'Him who is'" (God and Philosophy, London, 1941, p. 66).

Taking over this philosophy of Aristotle, St. Thomas was bound, in consequence, to "translate all the problems concerning being from the language of essences into that of existences." But could he do so without suppressing reason? Was it St. Thomas the theologian who, because of his faith, was able to make this transposition from the realm of abstract essences to that of existence? If it was, then no progress has been made in solving the problem of the relation of authority and reason. In fact the problem then seems to be more difficult than ever. For the God of Aristotle has then begun to appear to be quite different from the God of the Christian faith. Aristotle's god, it is admitted, has not created the world and does not know the world. If such a god is the natural outcome of the activity of reason when it is not enlightened by faith does it not seem as though faith will have to reverse the decisions of reason with respect to God? A philosophy that deals with essences only would seem to resemble a merry-go-round hovering above reality but never touching it. Yet according to Rome, St. Thomas the Christian theologian need not at all ask St. Thomas the autonomous philosopher to reverse his decisions on the fundamental question about the existence of God.

It would appear then that St. Thomas the theologian might appear with the God of Moses, the "he who is" in order to present him for acceptance to St. Thomas the philosopher. If the God of Moses, the Creator and controller of the world, is the one to be accepted by St. Thomas the philosopher, he must first be reduced from an existent God to a pure essence, from the "he who is" to the "it that is not." St. Thomas the philosopher is bound, by the principles of his reason, to bring the information given him by St. Thomas the theologian into orderly relation with the body of his beliefs about reality in general. And this involves the rejection of the existence of a God whose existence and knowledge cannot be thus related. There would seem to be no escape from the conclusion that if we start with autonomous reason and contend that it deals with essences only, the being which comes to expression through these essences is a being whose very existence is that of correlativity to the human mind. Kant and his followers were not illogical when they drew this conclusion. We cannot start with Aristotle without eventually falling prey to Kant.

Gilson seeks desperately to escape this conclusion. Like all Roman Catholic apologists he must at some time or other face this question as to how the "He who is" of Moses and the "it that is not" of Aristotle are related. He does so by arguing as follows: "Beyond a world where 'to be' is everywhere at hand, and where every nature can account for what other natures are but not for their common existence, there must be some cause whose very essence it is 'to be.' To posit such a being whose essence is a pure Act of existing, that is, whose essence is not to be this or that, but 'to be,' is also to posit the Christian God as the supreme cause of the universe" (God and Philosophy, p. 72). But this argument does not escape the dilemma just mentioned. The logical implication of the method of Aristotle is his "god," the "it that is not." That has been asserted by Gilson himself and it is clearly correct. That is the only god that is accessible to reason alone. Yet Gilson constantly speaks as though "the existence of one God, the sole Creator of the world" is also accessible to reason (Christianity and Philosophy, p. 60). And this God is supposed to be accessible to reason in the way that is shown in the quotation just given. But how can a god who is not and a God who is the Creator of the world both, be the logical implication of the true method of philosophy?

Yet it might seem that we have reached a position which involves the idea of absolute authority for at least one dimension of life. The order of faith and all that it contains is to be accepted purely on authority. Here then we seem to have reached the idea of absolute rather than expert authority. Before we have finished with the Roman Catholic view of the relation of authority to reason, however, there are further matters to be considered.

In the first place it has been noted how valiantly Gilson seeks to defend the idea of the autonomy of reason. If then the dimensions of reason and of faith are finally to be brought together into union with one another there will have to be a compromise. If there is one thing on which Roman Catholics insist, it is that only on their position is it possible to do justice to the statement of St. Paul that every man naturally knows something of God, without compromising the uniqueness of the Christian faith. In other words they maintain that it is in their system as a whole that there is a true union of the natural and the supernatural. But it is not difficult to see that if the autonomy of reason is to be maintained and the absolute authority of faith as well, any union between them must be one of compromise.

In the second place we may discover the nature of the compromise if we go back to the Roman Catholic conception of the nature of man, and especially of man's freedom in relation to God. According to Roman Catholic theology man has a measure of autonomy over against the plan of God. God has to await man's decisions on many points. Thus God does not really control whatsoever comes to pass. And this means that man's ultimate environment is only partly under God's direction. All of this implies, in effect, that on the basis of Roman Catholic theology there is mystery for God as well as for man. God himself is therefore on this basis surrounded by brute fact. Man's dealings are partly with God but also partly with brute fact. It is no wonder then that holding this doctrine of the ultimacy of the mind and will of man in its theology, Romish theology should recognize the legitimacy of the idea of autonomy in the field of philosophy. Even when it speaks of Christian philosophy, as Gilson does, it must still base this philosophy upon the idea of autonomy. And even when it speaks of the original perfection of man when his reason was not "wounded" Rome still holds to the idea of autonomy for the mind and will of man to some extent. In all stages and in all respects of its thinking it is committed to this idea. In all stages and in all respects it is therefore also committed to the idea of brute fact as a part of man's ultimate environment.

Now it is this fact that Rome is always and everywhere committed to the idea of brute fact as such, to eventuation apart from the counsel of God, that is all-determinative on the question of its conception of the relation of reason to authority. Rome simply has not the materials with which to build a really Christian concept of authority. A truly Christian concept of authority presupposes that in all he does man is face to face with the requirement of God. But how could man be face to face with the requirement of God if God does not own and control all things? How could God face man with his requirements there where he has no power to rule? It is only on the idea of the comprehensiveness of the plan of God that a true concept of authority can be based. And this is to say, in effect, that only on the idea of the covenant as all-comprehensive with respect to every phase of human life can the idea of authority find a footing.

Our conclusion then is that while the Roman Catholic notion of authority seems at first sight to be very absolute — in fact even more absolute than that of Protestantism — it is in reality not absolute at all. Its idea of autonomy wins out in every case. And so it comes to pass that the Roman Catholic doctrines of faith are in every instance adjusted to the idea of human autonomy. To be sure, the natural man is said to be fallen, but he has fallen but a little way; even in the state of rectitude he justly insisted on autonomy. Does the fallen character of man consist in his using this autonomy unwisely? To be sure, the Christian man is healed by grace; but even when he is healed he is still advised to exercise his autonomous will to some extent over against the plan of God. The concept of covenant obedience does not fit in anywhere in Roman Catholic theology or philosophy. Our conclusion must therefore be that even Rome offers nothing in the way of authority that is clearly different from the idea of the expert as this is willingly granted by the natural man.

The Roman Catholic concept of tradition only corroborates what has been said. In its "Decree concerning the canonical Scriptures" the Council of Trent speaks of "unwritten traditions" which are as it were transmitted from hand to hand. These unwritten traditions are accorded the same authority as Scripture. Christian truth, it is said, has come to us by way of two distinct streams, one of which is found in Scripture and the second of which is found in tradition. To be sure this tradition may, to some extent at least, be itself reduced to writing. Yet there is no body of writings which the church officially accepts as containing the written statement of what it accepts as tradition. It is the living voice of the Church speaking in its official ministers, and especially through the Pope, that is the final guardian of this tradition. Tradition is therefore finally that which the church propounds from time to time.

The bearing of this conception of tradition on the questions of authority and its relation to reason must now be drawn. The hierarchy of the church in general, and of the Pope in particular, is not to be thought of as itself subject to the final and comprehensive revelation of God. There is no place anywhere in the whole of Roman Catholic thought for the idea that any human being should be wholly subject to God. On the contrary, the position of Rome requires the rejection of the counsel of God as all-determinative. Hence the Pope himself, as he makes up his mind with respect to the infallible pronouncement that his office requires or permits him to make from time to time, must seek as an expert to interpret the meaning of brute fact, of being in general. What the Bible teaches him he will be required to relate to what his autonomous reason teaches him with respect to being in general. The result is that the voice of God as the controller and governor of man and the universe can never speak through the voice of the Pope. Those who listen to the voice of the Pope are listening to the voice of an expert who is supposed, for some wholly non-rational reason, to be able to peer more deeply into the realm of "Being" than other men are able to.

It appears then, that so far from being the defender of the true Christian concept of authority and of reason, Rome offers a compromise both on ideas and therefore on the relation between them. Holding to a concept of reason that is not itself interpreted in terms of the doctrine of God as self-contained it can offer no concept of authority that really stands above reason. Its authority therefore is the galling authority of one man dealing with "being in general'' and guessing about it, over another man also dealing with ''being in general'' and guessing about them. It is the authority that brings men into bondage.

The entire position of Rome then with respect to authority and its relations to reason illustrates the weakness of Roman Catholic apologetics in general. It has no clear cut position that can be contrasted with that of the natural man. It cannot therefore challenge the position of the natural man with any effectiveness at any point. Assuming the correctness of the starting point and the method of the natural man in the natural sphere it cannot logically ask men to accept the authority of God even in the spiritual sphere.

Arminianism

It will appear to many as a very strange thing to say that Arminian theology is similar to that of Romanism on the question of authority. Yet this is really the case. Of course it is true that evangelical Arminians reject the ritualism and the hierarchy of Rome. It is also true that individual Arminians are much better in their practical attitude toward Scripture than their system of theology permits them to be. It is only of this system of theology that we speak. And of it — there is no escape from it — the assertion must be made that its conception of reason is similar to that of Rome and therefore its conception of authority cannot be very different from that of Rome.

There is nothing on which Arminian theology is more insistent than that the Reformed doctrine of election does injustice to man's responsibility. Yet the Reformed doctrine of election is but the consistent expression in the field of man's relation to God of the general teaching of Scripture that all things in history happen by the plan of God. The Arminian doctrine of responsibility therefore presupposes the rejection of the idea of the plan of God as all-inclusive. And this means that the idea of brute fact is one of the basic ingredients of the Arminian position. Man is therefore once again partly related to God and partly to some form of ''being in general.'' And this in turn means that God himself is confronted with that which determines his powers and actions. He is limited by the facts of Reality about him and his knowledge is accordingly surrounded by mystery.

Thus we are back at that arch foe of Christianity, namely, the idea of human ultimacy or autonomy. This idea of autonomy expresses itself in modern times by holding that in all that comes to man he gives as well as takes. Modern philosophy has, particularly since the day of Kant, boldly asserted that only that is real for man which he has, in part at least, constructed for himself.

Nor is this modern form of manifestation of the would-be autonomous man illogical. In every non-Christian concept of reality brute facts or chance play a basic role. This is so because any one who does not hold to God's counsel as being man's ultimate environment, has no alternative but to assume or assert that chance is ultimate. Chance is simply the metaphysical correlative of the idea of the autonomous man. The autonomous man will not allow that reality is already structural in nature by virtue of the structural activity of God's eternal plan. But if reality is non-structural in nature, man is the one who for the first time, and therefore in an absolutely original fashion, is supposed to bring structure into reality. But such a structure can be only "for him." For, in the nature of the case, man cannot himself as a finite and therefore temporally conditioned being, control the whole of reality. But all this amounts only to saying that modern philosophy is quite consistent with its own principles when it contends that in all that man knows he gives as well as takes. It is merely the non-rational that is given to him; he himself rationalizes it for the first time. And so that which appears to him as rationally related reality is so related primarily because he himself has rationalized it.

The modern form of autonomy expresses itself then both in a negative and in a positive fashion. Negatively it assumes or asserts that that which is "out there," that is, that which has not yet come into contact with the human mind, is wholly non-structural or non-rational in character. We are not now concerned so much to point out that this assumption is itself not very reasonable to make for one who claims to limit his assertions to what human experience can control. Human experience can hardly establish the universal negative assertion about the whole of reality and therefore about all future eventuality that is implied in the assumption of the average modern philosopher or scientist. What it is our main concern, however, to point out now is that the Arminian theologian is not in a good position to challenge this modern man in his attitude toward the authority of Scripture.

What is the attitude toward the idea of Scripture that we would expect to find on the part of modern man? Will it readily accept the idea? Will it be open-minded with respect to the "evidence" for the scriptural teaching with respect to such doctrines as creation, providence, and miracles? Will it be open-minded with respect to revelation given about future eventuation? That is to say, will it be ready to accept information about that which happens in a realm totally beyond human experience or what has happened, does happen and will happen by way of influence from that realm that is totally beyond human experience upon the realm of human experience? The answer is obvious. The entire idea of inscripturated supernatural revelation is not merely foreign to but would be destructive of the idea of autonomy on which the modern man builds his thought. If modern man is right in his assumption with respect to his own autonomy then he cannot even for a moment logically consider evidence for the fact of the supernatural in any form as appearing to man. The very idea of God as self-contained is meaningless on his principles. The idea of such a God, says the modern follower of Kant, is fine as a limiting notion. Taken as a limiting notion it is quite innocent and even useful. For then it stands merely for the ideal of exhaustive rationality. And science requires such an ideal. But the idea of such a God as taken by orthodox Christians, that is as a constitutive rather than as a limiting concept, is meaningless; it would kill the idea of pure fact as the correlative to pure rationality. And the idea of pure fact as a limiting concept is as necessary to modern science as is the idea of pure rationality.

It is therefore logically quite impossible for the natural man, holding as he does to the idea of autonomy, even to consider the "evidence" for the Scripture as the final and absolutely authoritative revelation of the God of Christianity. It is logically impossible for him to say anything about the revelation of such a God in the universe and to the mind of man. The God of Christianity is for him logically irrelevant to human experience. It would therefore be as sensible to talk about his revealing himself either in nature or in Scripture as it would be to ascribe to the man in the moon the perpetration of some murder in one's neighborhood.

This way of putting the matter may seem to some to be extreme. Yet we believe it to be strictly in accord with the facts. There are, to be sure, some among modern philosophers, particularly those of the theistic and personalist schools, who seem to be favorably disposed to what they call a positive religion. And among the positive religions they will pick out Christianity as the most acceptable. Mention may again be made of A.E. Taylor. In his recent book Does God Exist? Taylor argues for "the existence of God." But since he works on the assumption of the autonomy of man, the kind of God he believes in is, after all, a finite deity. When he deals with the tenets of historic Christianity Taylor makes perfectly clear that, on his principles, one could not accept them as being what they are presented as being in Scripture. Speaking of the resurrection of Jesus he says: "That St. Paul and the other Apostles believed this is as certain as any fact of past history can be; it is quite another question whether that belief was not a mistaken interpretation of their experiences. Since it is a familiar fact that men do sometimes misinterpret their experience, there is nothing in principle irrational in the suggestion that St. Paul and the other Apostles did this, and no man can prove 'beyond all shadow of doubt' that they did not" (London, 1947, p. 127). Taylor simply assumes that every human mind, that of an apostle no less than that of any other man, contributes in an original sense to what it receives. The result is that even if he could believe in a self-contained God – which on his premises he cannot – Taylor cannot believe that any man could receive any revelation from such a God without to some extent, in the very act of reception, confusing it with his own experiences that operate independently of this God.

The whole attitude of the modern man with respect to the idea of authoritative revelation such as is given in Scripture may therefore be summed up in the following points. Such a God as Scripture speaks of simply does not exist. This idea of the non-existence of God is involved, as has been noted, in the assumption of brute factuality. In the second place, if such a God did exist he could not manifest himself in the world that we know. For that world is known to be something other than the revelation of God; it is known to be a combination of brute factuality and the rationalizing activity of autonomous man with respect to them. In the third place, even if such a God did reveal himself in such a world as is known to be something other than a manifestation of him, no man could receive such a revelation without falsifying it. In the fourth place, if in spite of these three points a revelation had been received in the past it could not be transmitted to men of the present time without their again falsifying it. In the fifth place, if in spite of everything such a revelation of such a God as the Bible speaks of came to man today he in turn could not receive it without falsifying it.

Now Arminianism has no valid argument for the idea of biblical authority with which to challenge the position of modern man. Its own concept of man, as acting independently of the plan of God, to some extent, and therefore its own view of the human mind as being ultimate in some respects, paralyzes its apologetical efforts. Like the Roman Catholic, the Arminian apologist is bound to start with his opponent on a supposedly common basis. The Arminian must grant that his opponent has rightly interpreted much of human experience in terms of the autonomy of the human mind and the ultimacy of chance. But if the natural man who works with the idea of autonomy can correctly interpret the phenomenal world aright without God, why should he be ready to turn about suddenly and interpret spiritual things in terms of God? If he is consistent with himself he will not do so.

As has been noted earlier, the Arminian is bound to present the Christian position in atomistic fashion. He will therefore first speak to the non-believer about the possibility of supernatural revelation as though the word possibility meant the same thing for the natural man and for the believer. But it does not. For the natural man the idea of possibility is on the one hand identical with chance and on the other hand with that which the natural man himself can rationalize. For him only that is practically possible which man can himself order by his logical faculties. But the word possibility means for the Christian that which may happen in accord with the plan of God.

Secondly the Arminian may speak to the natural man of the probability of supernatural revelation as though the word probability meant the same thing for the believer and for the non-believer. But it does not. For the non-believer the meaning of the word probability is involved in his concept of the idea of possibility as just before discussed. Therefore, as Hume has effectively shown in his criticism of the empirical probability argument for Christianity, there can be no presumption at all for the eventuation of certain things rather than of others, once one allows the idea of chance in his system at all. There can be no probability that God will supernaturally reveal himself to man unless it is certain that without the presupposition of such a revelation man's experience, even of the realm of natural things, is meaningless.

In the third place the Arminian will speak to the natural man about the historical fact of revelation as recorded in Scripture. He will stress the fact that Christianity is a historical religion. To that he will add that therefore it is simply a matter of evidence whether or not, say, the resurrection of Christ, is a fact. On this question, he will insist, anybody who is able to use the canons of historical study is as good a judge as any other. "The meaning of the resurrection is a theological matter, but the fact of the resurrection is a historical matter..." (Wilbur Smith, Therefore Stand, p. 386). The proof for the resurrection is then said to be just the sort of proof that men demand everywhere in questions of history.

But this argument about the facts of supernatural revelation again forgets that the natural man's entire attitude with respect to the facts that are presented to him will naturally be controlled by his notions of possibility and probability as already discussed. He may therefore grant that a man named Jesus of Nazareth arose from the dead. He need not hesitate, on his principles, to accept the fact of the resurrection at all. But for him that fact is a different sort of fact from what it is for the Christian. It is not the same fact at all. It is in vain to speak about the fact without speaking of the meaning of the fact. For the factness of the fact is to any mind that deals with it that which he takes it to mean. It is his meaning that is the fact to him. And it is impossible even to present the fact for what it really is, namely, that which it is according to its interpretation as given in Scripture, to the natural man, if one does not challenge his notions of possibility and probability that underlie his views of the facts of history. To talk about presenting to him the fact of the resurrection without presenting its true meaning is to talk about an abstraction. The resurrection either is what the Christian says it is, or it is not. If it is, then it is as such that it actually appears in history.

Yet the Arminian position is committed to the necessity of presenting the facts of Christianity as being something other than he himself as a Christian knows they are. He knows that it is the Son of God who died in his human nature and rose again from the dead. But the fact of the resurrection about which he speaks to unbelievers is some nondescript something or other about which believers and non-believers are supposed to be able to agree.

In the fourth place, then, the Arminian will speak to the unbeliever about the Bible as the inspired and infallible revelation of God. He will argue that it is the most wonderful book, that it is the best seller, that all other books lose their charm while the Bible does not. All of these things the unbeliever may readily grant without doing any violence to his own position and without feeling challenged to obey its voice. It means to him

95

merely that some experts in religion have somehow brought to expression some of the deep fellow feeling with Reality that they have experienced. Their position allows for sacred books and even for a superior book. But the one thing it does not allow for is an absolutely authoritative book. Such a book presupposes the existence and knowability of the self-contained God of Christianity. But such a God, and the revelation of such a God in the universe and to man, are notions that, as has already been observed, the natural man must reject. So he will naturally also reject that which is simply the logical implicate, of the idea of such a God and of such a revelation. The very idea of sin, because of which the idea of an externally promulgated supernatural revelation of grace became imperative, is meaningless for him. For him sin or evil is a metaphysical action that is inherent in the concept of Chance.

The Reformed Position

Enough has now been said to indicate that the Roman Catholic and the Arminian methods, proceeding as they do by way of accepting the starting point and the method of the natural man with respect to a supposedly known area of experience, are self-refuting on the most important question of the Bible and its authority. We repeat that many Arminians are much better than their position. We also stress the fact that many of the things that they say about points of detail are indeed excellent. In other words our aim is not to depreciate the work that has been done by believing scholars in the Arminian camp. Our aim is rather to make better use of their materials than they have done by placing underneath it an epistemology and metaphysic which make these materials truly fruitful in discussion with non-believers.

Such a foundation it is that is furnished in the Reformed position. But it is furnished by the Reformed position simply because this position seeks to be consistently Christian in its starting point and methodology. And here it must be confessed that those of us who hold this position are all too often worse than our position. Those who hold the Reformed position have no reason for boasting. What they have received they have received by grace.

The Reformed position seeks to avoid the weaknesses of the Roman Catholic and the Arminian positions. Since these positions have now been discussed at length it will be immediately apparent what is meant. Since the natural man assumes the idea of brute fact in metaphysics and the idea of the autonomy of the human mind in epistemology, the Reformed apologist realizes that he should first challenge these notions. He must challenge these notions in everything that he says about anything. It is these notions that determine the construction that the natural man puts upon everything that is presented to him. They are the colored glasses through which he sees all the facts. Now Romanism and Arminianism also seek to present to the unbelievers the facts of Christianity. We have seen that in reality their own false interpretations of the facts of Christianity mean that they do not really present the facts fully for what they are. But to the extent that they do present the facts as they are, they still do not challenge the natural man to take off his colored glasses. And it is precisely this that the Reformed apologist seeks to do. He will first present the facts for what they really are and then he will challenge the natural man by arguing that unless they are accepted for what they are according to the Christian interpretation of them, no facts mean anything at all.

Here then are the facts, or some of the main facts that the Reformed apologist presents to the natural man. There is first the fact of God's self-contained existence. Second, the fact of creation in general and of man as made in God's image in particular. Third, there is the fact of the comprehensive plan and providence of God with respect to all that takes place in the universe. Then there is the fact of the fall of man and his subsequent sin. It is in relation to these facts and only in relation to these facts that the other facts pertaining to the redemptive work of Christ, are what they are. Their very factness as facts would not be what it is unless the facts just mentioned are what they are. Thus there is one system of reality of which all that exists forms a part. And any individual fact of this system is what it is primarily because of its relation to this system. It is therefore a contradiction in terms to speak of presenting certain facts to men unless one presents them as parts of this system. The very factness of any individual fact of history is precisely what it is because God is what he is. It is God's counsel that is the principle of individuation for the Christian man. God makes the facts to be what they are.

To be sure, man's actions have their place in this system. But they are not ultimately determinative; they are subordinately and derivatively important. Hence the idea of human autonomy can find no place in the truly Christian system any more than can the idea of chance. The human being is analogical rather than original in all the aspects of its activity. And as such its activity is truly significant.

It is natural that only the supernatural revelation of God can inform man about such a system as that. For this system is of a nature quite different from the systems of which the natural man speaks. For him a system is that which man, assumed to be ultimate, has ordered by his original structural activity. The natural man virtually attributes to himself that which a true Christian theology attributes to the self-contained God. The battle is therefore between the absolutely self-contained God of Christianity and the would-be wholly self-contained mind of the natural man. Between them there can be no compromise.

The idea of supernatural revelation is inherent in the very idea of this system of Christianity which we are seeking to present to the natural man. But if this is so then the idea of a supernatural, infallibly inscripturated revelation is also inherent in this system. Man as the creature of God needs supernatural revelation and man, become a sinner, needs supernatural redemptive revelation. He needs this revelation in infallibly inscripturated form lest he himself destroy it. As a hater of God he does not want to hear about God. The natural man seeks to suppress the pressure of God's revelation in nature that is about him. He seeks to suppress the pressure of conscience within him. So he also seeks to suppress the idea of the revelation of grace that speaks in Scripture. In every case it is God as his Creator and as his Judge that asks of him to listen and be obedient. How can the autonomous man be obedient on his own assumptions? He cannot be obedient unless he reverses his entire position, and this he cannot do of himself. It takes the regenerating power of the Spirit to do that.

Having reached this point the Roman Catholic and the Arminian may argue that it was in the interest of avoiding this very impasse that they sought to make their point of contact with the natural man on a neutral basis. The reply of the Reformed apologist is as follows. Good preaching, he will say, will recognize the truth of Scripture that man has been blinded by sin, and that his will is perverted toward seeking self instead of God. But how can deaf ears hear, and blind eyes see? That is to say preaching is confronted with the same dilemma as is apologetical reasoning. In both cases the Roman Catholic and the Arminian tone down the facts of the gospel in order to gain acceptance for them on the part of the natural man. In neither case will the Reformed apologist do so. In both cases he will challenge the natural man at the outset. Both in preaching and in reasoning – and every approach to the natural man should be both – the Reformed theologian will ask the sinner to do what he knows the sinner of himself cannot do. The Reformed Christian is often to be Reformed in preaching and Arminian in reasoning. But when he is at all self-conscious in his reasoning he will seek to do in apologetics what he does in preaching. He knows that man is responsible not in spite of but just because he is not autonomous but created. He knows that the idea of analogical or covenant personality is that which alone preserves genuine significance for the thoughts and deeds of man. So he also knows that he who is dead in trespasses and sins is none the less responsible for his deadness. He knows also that the sinner in the depth of his heart knows that what is thus held before him is true. He knows he is a creature of God; he has been simply seeking to cover up this fact to himself. He knows that he has broken the law of God; he has again covered up this fact to himself. He knows that he is therefore guilty and is subject to punishment forever: this fact too he will not look in the face.

And it is precisely Reformed preaching and Reformed apologetic that tears the mask off the sinner's face and compels him to look at himself and the world for what they really are. Like a mole the natural man seeks to scurry under ground every time the facts as they really are come to his attention. He loves the darkness rather than the light. The light exposes him to himself. And precisely this neither Roman Catholic or Arminian preaching or reasoning are able to do.

As to the possibility and likelihood of the sinner's accepting the Christian position, it must be said that this is a matter of the grace of God. As the creature of God, made in the image of God, he is always accessible to God. As a rational creature he can understand that one must either accept the whole of a system of truth or reject the whole of it. He cannot understand why a position such as that of Roman Catholicism or of Arminianism should challenge him. He knows right well as a rational being that only the Reformed statement of Christianity is consistent with itself and therefore challenges the non-Christian position at every point. He can understand therefore why the Reformed theologian should accept the doctrine of Scripture as the infallible Word of God. He can understand the idea of its necessity, its perspicuity, its sufficiency and its authority as being involved in the Christian position as a whole.

But while understanding them as being involved in the position of Christianity as a whole, it is precisely Christianity as a whole, and therefore each of these doctrines as part of Christianity, that are meaningless to him as long as he is not willing to drop his own assumptions of autonomy and chance.

It follows that on the question of Scripture, as on every other question, the only possible way for the Christian to reason with the non-believer is by way of presupposition. He must say to the unbeliever that unless he will accept the presuppositions and with them the interpretations of Christianity there is no coherence in human experience. That is to say, the argument must be such as to show that unless one accept the Bible for what true Protestantism says it is, as the authoritative interpretation of human life and experience as a whole, it will be impossible to find meaning in anything. It is only when this presupposition is constantly kept in mind that a fruitful discussion of problems pertaining to the phenomena of Scripture and what it teaches about God in his relation to man can be discussed.